Bangkok

TOPOGRAPHICS

Bangkok

William Warren

REAKTION BOOKS

Published by Reaktion Books Ltd
79 Farringdon Road, London EC1M 3JU
www.reaktionbooks.co.uk

First published 2002

Printed and bound in Great Britain by
Biddles Ltd, Guildford and King's Lynn

British Library Cataloguing in Publication Data

Warren, William, 1930-
    Bangkok. – (Topographics)
    1. Bangkok (Thailand) – History 2. Bangkok (Thailand) – Social life
    and customs
    I. Title
    959.3

    ISBN 1 86189 129 6

Contents

Introduction

In the past, Bangkok nearly always proved elusive to foreign visitors recording their impressions, just as it does today. In part, this may have been because the majority tended to stay for a brief time, sometimes only a few weeks or even days, and experienced the city from a narrow vantage point — the splendour of a royal palace, for example, in the case of early emissaries, or the comforts of a luxury hotel; for many in more recent years, a smoky night spot fulfilling the most esoteric of sexual fantasies.

Some have viewed the city less as a real place than as an exotic image. 'We left London in ballast — sand ballast — to load a cargo of coal in a northern port for Bangkok,' says Marlow, the hero of Joseph Conrad's *Youth* (1898). 'Bangkok! I thrilled. I had been six years at sea, but had only seen Melbourne and Sydney, very good places, charming in their way — but Bangkok!' Despite this build-up, Marlow never reaches Bangkok in the story; his first ship is becalmed off England, while his second burns at sea off the coast of Java. Conrad himself did come as a 30-year-old seaman in 1888, to take up his first command, though he only described the city of his dreams in a perfunctory way in a later story. (Nevertheless, he is regarded as part of its literary history; a suite is named after him in the Author's Wing of the venerable Oriental Hotel, where he almost certainly never passed a night.)

Alone among the countries of South-east Asia, Siam managed, through diplomatic skill, geopolitics and pure luck, to retain its independence, and this quality of perceived isolation probably added both to Bangkok's allure and to the difficulty of getting a cultural grasp on it. Somerset Maugham,

7

who came in 1923 on one of his trawls for useful material, was bewildered at first. Bangkok seemed to him merely another big Asian city, indistinguishable from others he had seen in his travels. 'They are all alike,' he wrote in *The Gentleman in the Parlour* (1930),

> with their straight streets, their arcades, their tramways, their dust, their blinding sun, their teeming Chinese, their dense traffic, their ceaseless din. They have no history and no traditions. Painters have not painted them. No poets transfiguring dead bricks and mortar with their divine nostalgia, have given them a tremulous melancholy not their own. They live their own lives, without associations, like a man without imagination. They are hard and glittering and as unreal as a backcloth in a musical comedy. They give you nothing.

Maugham was a perceptive traveller, however, and he followed this rather too mannered description with another thought:

> But when you leave them it is with a feeling that you have missed something and you cannot help thinking that they have some secret that they have kept from you. And though you have been a trifle bored you look back on them wistfully; you are certain that they have after all something to give you which, had you stayed longer or under other conditions, you would have been capable of receiving. For it is useless to offer a gift to him who cannot stretch out a hand to take it.

Geoffrey Gorer, a decade later, had no such doubts about what he found. Pausing between the magic of Bali and the majesty of Angkor, he found it

> difficult to take Bangkok seriously. It is the most hokum place I have ever seen, never having been to California. It is

the triumph of the 'imitation' school; nothing is what it looks like; if it's not parodying European buildings, it is parodying Khmer ones; failing anything else, it will parody itself.

Another visiting author, just after the Second World War, *had* been to California, but took a more generous view. 'From the very beginning,' wrote S. J. Perelman *in Westward Ha!* (1948),

I was charmed by Bangkok and I propose to be aggressively syrupy about it in the most buckeye travelogue manner . . . Its character is complex and inconsistent; it seems at once to combine the Hannibal, Missouri of Mark Twain's boyhood with Beverly Hills, the Low Countries and Chinatown.

Paul Theroux, in *The Great Railway Bazaar* (1975), was struck by a darker aspect, one that has come to predominate in more contemporary impressions: 'As Calcutta smells of death and Bombay of money, Bangkok smells of sex, but this sexual aroma is mingled with the sharper whiffs of death and money.'

J. R. Ackerley, whose *Hindoo Holiday* (1932) is a classic of travel literature, was particularly savage, perhaps because he came after a very happy visit to Japan where he fell in love with the culture and several of the inhabitants. 'Make a firm resolution never to come,' he wrote to the novelist Francis King, with whom he had stayed in Kyoto, and went on to explain why:

The heat is stunning and humid, the place is a network of mostly stagnant waterways, all breeding mosquitoes galore, the terrain is perfectly flat in all directions, a low skyline, no higher than the length of palms, and banana and rain-trees that hem one in. Moving away from dear Japan towards India, all the disagreeable features of that latter country, as I remember it, begin here: the muddy complexion (often diddy-daddied), the muddy eye, laziness, stupidity, dishonesty, betel-chewing, dirt and filthy smells, bad and unhygienic food, no hot water, prickly heat, rampant rabies, and wretched, mangy dogs, hairless and emaciated, whom no one will kill and no one will feed. You would *detest* it, my dear.

At least one noted writer, Paul Bowles, gave up before he even tried. Though Bowles briefly owned a tiny island off the coast of Sri Lanka, he was primarily associated with North Africa, and it is hard to see why his American publisher thought that he and Bangkok would be a comfortable fit. Nevertheless, Bowles accepted a commission to write a book about the city, arriving in the mid-1960s with the intention of spending several months doing research. He stayed about two weeks, loathed most of what he saw (not much since he seldom left his hotel room) and then abandoned the project. The task was passed on to Alec Waugh, who liked the place and had friends there, but who produced a bland account, largely assembled, it seems, from various published sources. It concludes with the following summary:

> No place remains the same for ever. But Bangkok has been loved because it is the expression of the Thais themselves, of their lightheartedness, their love of beauty, their reverence for tradition, their sense of freedom, their extravagance, their devotion to their creeds – to characteristics that are constant and continuing in themselves. Bangkok has always been that; I think that it will stay that way; I do not believe it can be spoiled.

None of these literary views, it seems safe to say, would be very meaningful to the ten million or so Thais who live in the city. (That's the official figure. Nobody knows the true one, for the simple reason that a vast number are registered as living in their home provinces, which might be hundreds of kilometres away.) Nor, probably, would it be meaningful to most of the foreigners who have chosen, for a wide variety of reasons, to make their home here. They each have their own personal view, favourable or not, determined in large part by where they live, what they do, what they like.

I got my own introduction in the spring of 1959. Spring, that is, to the Western world; in Bangkok, it was the middle of the hot season, when the whole city becomes an enormous moist oven, and every movement outdoors is a major effort. I was working for an American documentary-film company that had vague ideas of filming something here, and I was supposed to move around a good deal, meeting various people, seeing all of the major sights, gathering material for use in a script (which, as it happened, never got written).

I gave up serious sightseeing quite soon, in a kind of despair. One of the people I met kindly arranged a temporary membership at the Royal Bangkok Sports Club, and I spent most of the day there, by the swimming pool, or locked in my cheap but air-conditioned room at a hotel that turned out to be a part-time brothel. Sometimes, though, when the heat of the day subsided and a relatively cool breeze stirred the trees in the nearby park, I ventured out and went by pedicab to see some of the things I'd read about in guidebooks. I saw the royal palace and some of the more noted Buddhist temples; I went to a market or two; I attended a performance of classical dance, presented in a stifling shed with a tin roof; I was a guest at the first party held in Jim Thompson's famous Thai-style house, filled with his dazzling art collection.

Bangkok dazed me, in a way no other city ever had or has since. I could not associate it with a definite mood, a distinctive personality. It seemed endless, mile after mile of low, drab, ugly row shops, spilling dusty wares out on the sidewalks in blinding sunlight. The names of streets, even when printed in English letters (as most of them are), were immensely long, unpronounceable, impossible to remember. Ratchadamnoen, Ratchadamri, Bamrungmuang: how could any newcomer even begin to get through such tongue-twisters and communicate with a taxi driver? Away from New Road and a few of its side streets – then the tourist centre – I never quite knew where I was. The local people I met were unfailingly polite, but, except for those at the Sports Club, I could usually not understand what they were saying to me; incredible as it seems to me today, I did not even find them particularly attractive to look at. I felt, acutely, all the discomforts of being in a strange place where I could not speak the language, where the culture was elusive and where the climate discouraged any great effort to do much about either.

Yet exactly a year later, I was on a Dutch freighter, coming from New York with every intention of making my home in Bangkok.

Why? What happened in that short interval to alter my perceptions? Even now, I can't offer a clear answer. In part, it was personal, a sudden overwhelming need (stronger than a mere desire) to completely change the direction of my life. But, more than that, I wanted specifically to go to Bangkok. Somehow, those confusing first impressions had coalesced into a desirable destination, as vague in a way as Conrad's image, but nevertheless as tantalizing as the gift Maugham failed to accept. Undoubtedly, I had missed something; people I had met and liked, like Jim Thompson, had fallen under the city's spell and intended to spend their lives there; maybe it would offer me the same kind of fulfilment, fulfilment I had not found elsewhere.

I realize that none of this really explains a decision to jettison most of my worldly belongings, leave friends and family, and move to a place on the other side of the world, but it is the best I can do. And within a few days of disembarking at Klong Toey Port and settling into my first house, I knew I had made the right choice.

Perhaps telling the story of Bangkok, and some of the things I have gradually learned about it over the years, will make my reasons clearer to others.

1 Bangkok in Time

For a century or so, Bangkok's development was largely the result of royal dreams, aspirations and, occasionally, eccentric whims, in particular those of the first six rulers of the Chakri dynasty. Known as Lords of Life and ruling (at least theoretically) with absolute authority, they were responsible for the city's original layout and architectural forms, as well as for the art that adorned its earliest buildings and the laws that governed its people. Many of their contributions survive and, while physically now only a small part of the sprawling whole, still play a significant symbolic role in Thai life.

It was the first Chakri King, known in Thai history as Rama I, who chose the site of the capital in 1782 to celebrate the beginning of a hopeful new era. Successive members of the dynasty made the major decisions on expansions and additions until 1932, when the absolute monarchy came to a surprisingly peaceful end.

As a place, though, Bangkok had existed long before the dynasty. For several centuries, first as a small village and later as a sizeable trading port, it had been a major stop on the busy river route to Ayutthaya, the glittering, cosmopolitan capital a little further upstream.

The city's name derives from *bang*, meaning village, and *kok*, a species of wild plum (*Spondias pinnata*) that apparently grew in some quantity along the river. It began to appear on maps made by the Portuguese shortly after their first official contact with Ayutthaya in 1511. Later that century, an Ayutthaya King raised Bangkok's status to that of a town, at the same time changing its name to Thon Buri. However, Europeans persisted in calling it Bangkok, as they would even after it became the capital and was given another, far more elaborate title; Thon Buri eventually came to refer only to the settlement on the west bank. To reduce travel time for ships coming up from the Gulf of Thailand, the same King had a two-kilometre canal dug across a long loop in the river at this point; erosion over the years eventually widened the canal until it became the main course, passing beside today's Grand Palace.

According to European missionaries in the seventeenth century, Bangkok was actually a collection of villages noted for their plantations of tall betel-nut palms. The main village, with the governor's house, was on the west bank of the Chao Phraya. The site was strategic, 'the only place that could offer some resistance to enemy attack', according to Nicholas Gervaise, and two forts were built for this purpose, one on each bank.

A grand embassy dispatched by King Louis XIV stopped in Bangkok in October 1685, part of what would prove to be an ill-fated effort to establish a strong French presence in what was then known as Siam (the country's name was changed to Thailand in the 1930s). With the party was the Abbé de Choisy, a rather unlikely ecclesiastic (in his earlier life, he had been a noted Parisian transvestite), who observed with approval the splendidly carved royal barges sent to greet the visitors and the profusion of wildlife in the surrounding countryside. 'There are many animals in this land,' he wrote, 'because people dare not kill them in case they kill their father; metempsychosis is an article of faith among the Siamese.' Three years later, the dreams of the French ended in a bloody revolt led by court conservatives, and their soldiers were back in Bangkok, this time fighting for their lives in the east-bank fort until a truce allowed them (and most other Westerners) to leave Siam for the better part of a century.

In 1767 the worst disaster in Thai history came with the fall of Ayutthaya to an invading army from Burma. There had been defeats before, followed by relatively benign occupations, but this time the Burmese were ruthless. They put the great city to the torch, burning most of its fabled Buddhist temples and palaces, looting its treasures and scattering its demoralized population into the countryside to starve. This catastrophe would haunt the Thais for generations and would strongly influence the history of Bangkok.

Out of the confusion emerged a charismatic leader of Chinese descent, who, within a year, had rallied his people, expelled the Burmese and established himself as King Taksin. Taksin made his headquarters at Thon Buri and began to build a capital there – a palace near the old fort with an adjacent royal *wat*, or Buddhist temple – but for the next decade, most of his energies were expended on consolidating his power and adding to his territory. By 1782, his behaviour had become increasingly eccentric, and many in the court were convinced he had lost his mind. There was again a palace revolt; the King was overthrown and, in due course, executed in the manner prescribed for royalty by Ayutthaya law: he was placed in a velvet sack and beaten to death with a sandalwood club.

The popular choice for Taksin's successor was another military figure, Chao Phraya Chakri, who had distinguished himself by many victories, the most famous of which had been the capture of Vientiane in present-day Laos. From there, he had brought back one of the greatest treasures of the region, a legendary nephrite image known as Phra Keo, or the Emerald Buddha, originally found in the far north in the fifteenth century. The image had been kept in various northern cities, principally Chiang Mai, until 1552, when it had been taken to Vientiane to save it from the Burmese.

Chakri was off fighting again, this time in Cambodia, when he heard of events in Thon Buri and hastened back. Legend has it that he marched down what is now called Chetupon Road – a narrow thoroughfare that separates the two parts of Wat Phra Chetupon (Wat Po) – on 6 April 1792. That same day, after crossing the river, he was offered and accepted the crown, thus inaugurating a new dynasty bearing his name. (Chakri Day is celebrated every year on 6 April, and tribute is paid to some of his ashes at Wat Phra Chetupon.)

One of Chakri's first decisions was to move the capital across to Bangkok. There were several good reasons for doing so, both practical and psychological. From a military standpoint, Bangkok could be defended more easily, with the river serving as a natural defence on one side and, on the other, a swampy plain known as the Sea of Mud, which extended almost to the Gulf of Thailand. (Today, one of Bangkok's most exclusive residential districts is located on this plain, and it is still subject to frequent floods in the rainy season.) Symbolically, too, a change seemed advisable; Thon Buri was too closely associated with the previous reign, the palace area was too small and unimpressive, and a new city would proclaim the aspirations of a new dynasty.

These aspirations were hardly modest. They called for the virtual recreation of lost Ayutthaya, to the point of duplicating as closely as possible many of its well-remembered palaces and temples as well as its physical layout. Thus an old canal was enlarged and extended to form an artificial island at a point where the river bent sharply, and a new one, fortified by a high wall, was dug farther to the east. The new city wall was 3.6 m high, dotted with sixteen gates and sixteen forts, and built partially with stones brought down on barges from the old capital.

Within this area, known today as Rattanakosin Island, the King proposed to erect a palace for himself, another for the Second King, who acted as a sort of vice-ruler (the institution was abolished in the reign of Rama V), and a splendid temple for the sacred Emerald Buddha. Other temples would also be built to gain merit and old ones like Wat Phra Chetupon restored for the same reason. Part of the site was occupied by a prosperous Chinese trading community that was relocated about 3 km to the south, outside the walls but still on the river. Continuing its business, this became the nucleus of Bangkok's Chinatown and for the next two centuries – to some extent, even today – the centre of the town's economic power.

A view within the Grand Palace grounds, *c.* 1900.

Construction of the Grand Palace took three years, with the King himself, it is said, living on the site in a simple wooden house to supervise the small army of labourers. Prince Chula Chakrabongse, a descendant of Rama I who wrote a history of the dynasty, points out that while these workers were conscripted for the task,

> it is unlikely that they suffered great hardship. They were fed at the royal expense by a communal kitchen, and some might have had better and more food than at home. If there was hardship, some of the stories would have survived. But even if we grant that forced labour, with threats of punishment, was employed for the building of the new capital, the architects, craftsmen, and skilled artisans who embellished these buildings, could not be coerced by fear into producing such beautiful works of art. Judging by what we can see today, even if a lot of it has been restored, these men must

17

have been profoundly inspired and stirred by love for Rama I himself as much as for the glory of Thai culture, to have accomplished so much of it in the space of three years.

Stirred by love or not, what they produced was an authentic wonder, and remains one today. Even outsiders who find it a bit over-the-top (no Thai ever would) are invariably stunned by the sheer quantity of gilt and glass mosaic, the swooping multi-tiered roofs and tall spires rising everywhere, a creation that seems even more fantastic in modern Bangkok than in the earlier city that produced it, at a time when such buildings were more common.

Like the Forbidden City of Beijing, and specifically like the royal palace of Ayutthaya, the Grand Palace was much more than the residence of the King. The compound originally covered an area of 21 hectares – another 3.5 hectares were added to the south by Rama II in 1809 – and faced north, the most auspicious direction, with the Chao Phraya on the right. The surrounding high walls had seventeen gates, the principal one being Pratu Wiset Chaisi, the 'Gate of Glorious Victory', in the centre of the north wall. Within were several clearly defined areas, an outer one that contained the civil and military head-quarters, a central one with the King's living quarters and the audience halls where he received visitors and presided over royal ceremonies, and another, well-guarded quarter for the female members of the royal family and their attendants, who steadily increased in number over the years. Elsewhere in the compound was the royal chapel, formally known as Wat Phra Sriratana Sasadaram, but more usually called Wat Phra Keo, the Temple of the Emerald Buddha.

In the words of Prince Chula, 'the palace was the very core and centre of the capital and indeed of the whole country.' On its completion in 1785, there were celebrations lasting three days, during which pavilions serving free food were set up in

The Emerald Buddha Temple.

the area and monks chanted prayers from the heart-shaped battlements on the city walls. The Emerald Buddha ceremonially crossed the Chao Phraya and was installed in its new home, conferring immense merit on both the King and his subjects.

Just outside the palace walls was a large open field, Sanam Luang, which became the place where royal cremations and other ceremonies were held. At one end, Rama I installed the Lak Muang, or city pillar, which is to be found in every old provincial capital and generally marks a city's exact geographical centre. This was a Brahmin custom, inherited, like much else involving royalty, from the Khmers; the pillar was supposed to enshrine the city's guardian spirit. Ever since its installation, the Lak Muang has been an important place for worship by the people of Bangkok, who come asking for everything from success in business to a winning ticket in the national lottery.

Ceremony at Sanam Luang, with the Palace in the foreground.

A Bangkok canal scene.

As a final act, the King bestowed an impressive new title on his capital, one so filled with honorifics that it qualifies as the longest city name in the world. Thais shorten it to Krung Thep, which can be roughly translated as 'city of divinities or angels', while foreigners (and most foreign map makers) have continued to use the old village name.

At the beginning, then, Bangkok was basically a medieval Thai city, a fortified island surrounded by smaller communities that arose to satisfy its needs for food, various crafts and manual labour. Water was the dominant element, as it had been in Ayutthaya. Though there were elephants, horses and oxen, and rough roads for them to travel along, nearly all long-distance communication was by way of the great river and along an increasingly intricate network of man-made canals, or *klongs*, that served as streets. An extraordinary variety of boats were used, ranging from simple canoes fashioned from hollowed-out tree trunks to magnificent royal barges as elaborately decorated as the palace and temple buildings.

These barges, another legacy from Ayutthaya, were originally designed as war ships and armed with cannons in the prow. As the threat of invasion subsided, they were used to carry the King about his capital as well as for *kathins*, annual merit-making ceremonies held at the end of the rainy season when robes and other gifts are presented to the monks of riverside temples. The French had been dazzled by such processions in the old capital – nearly all of their memoirs include a description – and so would the Westerners be who came to Bangkok during the nineteenth century.

Ordinary people lived in plain wooden houses outside the city walls, either raised up on posts as protection against floods or floating structures anchored along both banks of the river. Dense forest was quite near, cleared in some places for rice fields and fruit orchards, though as yet there was only a suggestion of the vast, abundant plains that would spread across the surrounding countryside.

The gulf was near the capital – considerably nearer then than now; accumulated silt has pushed it back over the years by 30-odd km – but relatively few ships called to trade at first. No Westerners were on hand to record Bangkok's construction or the ways of life within its massive walls. Yet as David K. Wyatt, the leading historian of Thailand, has pointed out, the city was hardly isolated from the outside world. Mural paintings of the period, while religious in theme, show crowds of what are obviously Bangkok residents, some of them Thai, but others belonging to different ethnic groups from neighbouring countries. 'This was no monolithic, homogeneous society, then,' Wyatt has said, 'but one with a good deal of diversity and vitality.'

Several more Burmese invasions had been repelled by the end of the eighteenth century. Siamese authority now extended over most of the territory that had been lost, and Bangkok, enjoying a period of stability, was poised to assume its proper place in the region.

As they had been in Ayutthaya, the Chinese were among the first to take advantage of the situation. Junks came up the Chao Phraya under their great, bat-wing sails, bringing luxury goods and precious metals to exchange for rice and forest products.

They arrived with the north-east monsoon in late January or early February and remained until June, when they left on the winds of the south-west monsoon. The royal court was the chief beneficiary of such trade, but the prosperity had a broader effect as well and attracted more people to the city.

Rama I died in September 1809 at the age of 72. He had been a man of extraordinary ability and considerable vision for his time. Unlike the kings of Ayutthaya, who, following the Khmer example, had been lofty, god-like figures seldom seen by their subjects, he was a recognizable human being, frequently going out to inspect the progress of his new capital and sharing power with his associates. Besides prowess on the battlefield, he also demonstrated an appreciation for the arts; literature, mural painting and the classical masked *khon* dance all flourished during his reign, and he participated in writing a revision of the Thai version of the Indian epic *Ramayana*.

One of Rama's greatest legacies was the fact that, for the first time in nearly a century, his death was followed by no bloody power struggle. He was peacefully succeeded by the eldest of his seventeen sons, thus ensuring continuity and further proclaiming the new dynasty's stability. (It should be pointed out here that under the Thai system, the eldest son did not automatically become King, the latter instead being chosen by an Accession Council from various possible candidates. More often than not in the past, this practice had led to conflict and sometimes to the elimination of whole families regarded as hostile to the winner).

Owing to Thai custom and new threats from Burma, Rama I's funeral was not held until eighteen months after his death. It was the first of many royal cremations held in the field outside the Grand Palace, a splendid event that blended solemn ritual with a carnival atmosphere in a distinctively Thai way. The King's body, in a golden urn, was carried out of the palace by 60 men on a palanquin and then transferred to a gilded chariot weighing over 20 tons. Prince Chula described the process:

To take the heavy urn from the palanquin to the top of the lofty coach, an open lift, worked by a pulley, had been invented . . . and it might well have been the first lift in the world. Many religious rites and alms-giving preceded the actual cremation. Offerings were made to no less than 10,000 monks, coins enclosed in lime fruits were thrown to the masses from eight points around the Phra Meru [pyre]. Clothing was distributed to the old and poor of over seventy years of age. There were open-air theatres, boxing matches, and colourful fireworks.

Farangs – the word signifying all Westerners, is of uncertain origin, some claiming it came from the Thai pronunciation of French, others that it was derived from Persian – had been largely absent from Siam since the late seventeenth century. A few remained; the Dutch, for instance, maintained a trading post at Ayutthaya almost until the end, Catholic missionaries ministered to a small number of converts, and an unknown number of Portuguese, or half-Portuguese (they had intermarried freely with local girls), were probably among the original settlers of Bangkok. In general, though, the kingdom was off the map as far as the newly expanding European powers were concerned – too remote, not rich enough (or so they thought) for exploitation.

This attitude began to change towards the end of the second reign. Having taken the island of Penang, off the coast of the Malay Peninsula, in 1785, the British came close to Rama I's southernmost territories; with the establishment of Singapore as a free port in 1819, trade became a more pressing issue. Towards the end of 1821, the British decided that some sort of negotiations were called for, and John Crawfurd, a Scot, was dispatched by the governor-general of British India to Bangkok.

Crawfurd was not the first Westerner to come on such a mission. A Portuguese, Carlos Manuel Silveira, had arrived a few years earlier from Macao. As he had not been sent by the King of Portugal, Rama II received him merely as a merchant.

But the meeting went off well because Silveira was willing to sell modern weapons. Thus he was warmly received, even given a royal title and a house on the river that subsequently, after many changes, became the Portuguese Embassy, the oldest in Bangkok today.

Crawfurd must have seemed an ideal choice. He had lived in Penang, where he had learned to speak Malay, as well as in Java during its brief period of British occupation; he had a reputation for being able to get along with 'natives' and adapt himself to foreign customs. But his experiences had been in places where foreign domination was established and more or less accepted; Siam offered a different challenge, and not for the first time, nor for the last, there was a clash of cultures that brought few benefits to either side.

'An eighteenth century gentleman rather lost in the nineteenth century world of commerce', as Michael Smithies has described him, Crawfurd found much to dislike in Bangkok. 'This people, of half-naked and enslaved barbarians,' he wrote later, 'have the hardihood to consider themselves the first nation in the world, and to view the performance of any servile office to a stranger as an act of degradation.' He had difficulty in finding suitable servants, his Malay was useless at the Thai court except through inadequate interpreters, negotiations were constantly interrupted by some royal funeral or other ceremony (perhaps invented to avoid some difficult decision); moreover, like so many Westerners at the court of the Chinese Emperor, he was deeply revolted by the custom of prostration in the presence of royalty, not just before the King but before lesser officials as well. In the end, nothing much was accomplished during the four months he spent in the city beyond gaining Thai recognition of British Penang, nearly 40 years after its settlement.

Crawfurd, however, wrote the first comprehensive account of the country since the ill-fated French venture, including the first views of early Bangkok that we have from a Western perspective. He noted the 'numerous winding creeks and canals' that served as streets and, around the palace area, a larger canal 'crowded with merchant-boats, loaded with rice, salt, cotton, dried fish, oil, dye-woods, etc.' The richness of the Buddhist temples impressed him, though not wholly in a favourable way. A bridge he passed under, for example,

> afforded a surprising example of the stupid inattention of a despotic Government and a superstitious people to all objects of public convenience and utility. The value of a very few of the brass images which we saw [in one of the temples], would have been sufficient to build a noble bridge at this place, where it was so much required; but the one which we now saw consisted of a single plank, and was elevated to the giddy height of at least thirty feet. The passengers, for safety, took hold of each others' hand as they passed along it.

Crawfurd provided the first mention of a curious structure in an open space outside Wat Suthat, one of Bangkok's most beautiful temples (Rama II himself is supposed to have worked on the exquisite carvings that adorn its doors). He described it as consisting of

> two enormous wooden-posts, or pillars, joined at the top by a cross-beam. Each of these pillars was certainly not less than seventy feet high, and in size equal to the main-mast of a ship of four or five hundred tons. Certain ceremonies of Buddhist worship, the nature of which I could not ascertain, are annually performed at this spot.

The ceremonies were, in fact, Brahmin rather than Buddhist. Many early visitors, and even a few later ones, got the two hopelessly confused, perhaps because they are so often blithely blended in Thai ritual, frequently with Hindu and animistic elements thrown in for good measure. Nonetheless, this was an accurate enough description of the Giant Swing, a Bangkok landmark that still stands today. Until the event was stopped in 1935, an annual festival was held in which daring young men mounted a swing between the two pillars and sought to seize with their teeth bags of money attached to bamboo poles of varying heights, the highest requiring the swing to make an arc of nearly 180 degrees while the assembled crowd held its breath.

Crawfurd offered, too, the first account of the immensely theatrical way in which early Bangkok rulers received emissaries from abroad. Such events were held in the Phra Thinang Amarin Winichai, the principal audience hall of the palace, and were carefully stage-managed for maximum effect. In the dim light, the King sat on a high throne, revealed only when a curtain was drawn after all the visitors were assembled below. 'He had more the appearance of a statue in a niche, than of a living being,' wrote Crawfurd. 'He wore a loose gown of gold tissue, with very wide sleeves. His head was bare, for he wore neither crown nor any ornament upon it.'

Rama II died in 1824 and was succeeded by Prince Chetsadabodin, one of his 38 sons. Some historians have claimed that the rightful heir should have been Prince Mongkut, whose mother had been accorded a higher royal status, but under the Thai system the matter was not quite so simple. Chetsadabodin had powerful supporters and would doubtless have won in any struggle; to avoid possible conflict, Mongkut went into the Buddhist monkhood, remaining there throughout the third reign, quietly preparing for the time when his exceptional talents would transform the kingdom.

Numerous Chinese-style buildings and ornaments had appeared within the palace compound during Rama II's time. These reflected changes that were taking place in the city as more and more immigrants, mostly from the poor southern provinces of China, came to share in Bangkok's growing opportunities. These newcomers settled at first in the area known as Chinatown, then – when this grew too congested – to the river's west bank, where more open land was available. They worked as coolies on the docks and as rickshaw pullers, established trading companies of all kinds, set up sawmills and warehouses and, since most of them were single men, gradually intermarried with local women to form an entirely new class of Sino-Thais whose children spoke Thai as their first language. According to David Wyatt, '[t]he best estimates indicate that the Chinese minority grew from about 230,000 in 1823 to 300,000 in 1850 and 792,000 in 1910; their proportion of the total population grew from less than 5 percent to 9.5 percent.' While they spread all over the country, especially the larger towns, by far the largest concentration was in Bangkok. As we shall see, they would have immense influence not only on the city's physical appearance but on its tastes and social life.

Smaller groups came from Burma, Laos, Malaya, Cambodia, Vietnam and India, often forming closely knit communities that retained their ethnic identity over many years. One of these, along the banks of Klong Mahanag near the present National Stadium, was called Ban Krua and was composed of Muslim Chams from Cambodia. Their traditional skills included silk weaving, and, clustered around their neighbourhood mosque, isolated by both race and religion, they continued working at their primitive looms long after weaving had become a vanished art elsewhere in the city. (They are still there today and just as tightly organized. When the Expressway Authority decided a few years ago to routinely appropriate some of their simple houses, as well as the mosque, to build an exit ramp, they rose up in furious protest. An effort to burn them out, a common enough procedure in other areas, was thwarted; armed vigilante groups patrolled the rickety boardwalks of the community, challenging outsiders after dark, and a campaign was launched in the local press. Eventually, the Authority was forced to admit defeat, and Ban Krua remains more or less as it was, with a few substantial new houses built by weavers who profited from the Thai silk boom after the Second World War.)

Non-Asians began to settle in the city as well, for a variety of reasons. Catholic missionaries, mostly Portuguese, had been active in Ayutthaya and built churches in the early years of Bangkok. Santa Cruz, on the west bank, was first erected in this period and twice rebuilt, in 1834 and 1913. The Church of the Immaculate Conception was established by French missionaries in the seventeenth century and rebuilt in 1837 by Bishop Jean-Baptiste Pallegoix, who resided there for a time. Having arrived early in the third reign, Pallegoix was a keen observer of the Thai scene and wrote one of the most perceptive accounts of the country and its culture. He enthusiastically described Bangkok as

> situated in the midst of boundless gardens consisting of luxuriant year-round growth. [It] makes a very picturesque sight; ships and a multitude of flag-bedecked junks cluster in rows at the edges of the two banks; golden spires, cupolas, and beautifully constructed lofty pyramids, embellished with designs of multi-coloured porcelain which soar into the air. The tiered roofs of the pagodas, ornamented with gold and covered with varnished tile, glitter as they reflect the rays of the sun. Thousands of shops floating in two rows are spread out before you, following the curved structure of a majestic river crossed in every direction by thousands of crafts, most of which are very elegant.

Like most other foreigners of the time, Pallegoix referred to the Chao Phraya as the Menam, sometimes spelled Meinam. In fact, this is the word used for all sizeable Thai rivers, as King Rama IV would feel obliged to point out to one of his later correspondents. (With little effect; 'Menam' continued to be used in accounts of the city for another century.)

The first two Protestant missionaries arrived in 1828, one English and the other German. Less sophisticated than their Catholic predecessors, they were also less charmed by the culture they encountered, awash (as they saw it) in ignorance,

Santa Cruz Church.

idolatry and such pernicious customs as polygamy; the very appearance of the Thais at the time – weird haircuts, exposed breasts, blackened teeth and stained lips (from chewing betel-nut) – seemed to proclaim their lack of virtue. Though they had some success with Chinese residents, who seemed to think that the Christian tracts they handed out contained the secrets of Western civilization, the Protestants never made many converts among the Thais. In other fields, however, some of them had a profound influence, none more so than Dr Dan Beach Bradley, who came in 1835.

Probably the best known Westerner who took up residence in nineteenth-century Siam was Anna Leonowens, though, as we shall see, both her credentials and her accomplishments were more imaginary than real. The story of Dr Bradley, which in some ways parallels hers, is not only true but also genuinely dramatic, even though it lacks those beguiling song cues and any hint of a romantic subplot. (Romance, indeed, seemed to play a very small part in Bradley's life; he courted both of his wives by mail, the second without having ever met her.)

Bradley and his first wife arrived from Singapore, where they had been forced to wait for six months before they could find a ship to take them on the final lap of a journey that had begun in Boston. Initial impressions were not encouraging:

When I rose on the first morning in Bangkok and took a glance of things around me, I could scarcely resist the sense of foreboding that assailed me. Oh how different, I thought, was the natural scenery here from what it was in Singapore. How gloomy the dwellings of the missionaries here when compared to the charming houses we had occupied on that attractive island . . . There was no prospect that seemed even the least cheering but the river, and that was so shut out from our view that we could see only a very little without walking out on an uninviting footpath to it. There was not even the slightest hill to be seen in any direction . . . There were some trees about the place, where thousands of crows came to roost at night. The kakawa, kakawa jargon they made in jabbering together in the early evening and morning was such that I had never dreamed of. This noise alone I could have borne without the thought of a murmur, but when united with the incessant jumbling of crickets, toads, and frogs, the barking and howling of dogs, and the snarling of cats, I confess that my missionary home seemed, for a little time, too horrible to endure.

But Bradley was secure in his faith, by nature an optimist, and he quickly overcame his despair and adjusted to life in the cacophonous city. During his first year, he treated more than 3,500 patients in his dispensary and performed Siam's first surgical operations; he later introduced vaccination against smallpox, as well as modern methods of childbirth. As one of his biographers has noted,

> Fame did not come to Bradley in the privacy of sterilized operating rooms under ideal conditions; it came on a simple table in the middle of his office. Privacy was an unknown luxury, for his operations, watched by a multitude of onlookers, served as Bangkok's version of a Hollywood extravaganza.

In 1844, Bradley started the *Bangkok Recorder*, Siam's first newspaper, and in 1858 he began to publish the *Bangkok Calendar*, to which King Rama IV contributed occasional articles. (Another influential friend was Chao Phraya Sri Suriyawong, who became regent when the young Prince Chulalongkorn succeeded to the throne in 1868.) He also got a more suitable house on the west bank, near the entrance to Klong Bangkok Yai in the old Portuguese settlement. It was a two-storey bungalow, with louvered shutters and verandas on all sides, a style that was becoming popular with foreign residents along the river and even with some Westernized Thais and Chinese. Bradley was particularly proud of his doors and windows, which he called 'a great improvement on all their predecessors, being many and large with posts plumb, and not leaning together or within after the then universal custom of Siam'. Bradley died, respected and showered with honours, in 1873; his second wife died twenty years later. Their daughter Irene, without a title deed but insisting that the property had been given to her father by the King, continued to live in the house until her own death in 1941, when the site was absorbed by the Royal Thai Navy, which had long had a claim to it. Only a little worse for wear, the house was still there, being used as a commissary, when I visited the navy compound in the 1970s. Nobody seemed to know that it had been built by the famous Dr Bradley or that it was, in a way, a pioneering specimen of architecture. It was unceremoniously torn down a few years later and replaced by a modern cement building.

Other foreigners came for the purpose of making money out of the new capital rather than saving souls. One of them was a Scot named Robert Hunter, who arrived shortly after Rama III's coronation and remained for twenty years, for much of that time the only British merchant resident in Bangkok. 'As a businessman,' a descendant has written,

[he] was shrewd and hard-headed, always with an eye to the main chance. As a person he was socially adaptable, with a persuasive tongue and the useful ability of 'getting in' with the right people. In Bangkok he became a partner in trade with the Government and had a certain amount of influence at Court. In many ways he was typical of the Westerner who adopted the East; he had money, he had power, and was thus inclined to throw his weight around, but he was without that bluff bonhomie so peculiar to the Englishman abroad. Instead, he had the studied reserve of the Scot, unless he was aroused, when a quick temper and an infuriating arrogance betrayed him.

33

A well-timed gift of a thousand muskets to assist in a struggle with Laos won Hunter the gratitude of Rama III, who in turn granted him a favour until then denied to any of the few Westerners living in the city. Since building plots were rare on the east bank of the river, reserved for royalty on the core island and otherwise limited to the already congested streets of Chinatown, Hunter had been forced to make his home on one of the houseboats anchored along the river. According to another foreign resident, F. A. Neale, who had accepted a post with the budding Thai navy, this was 'double the size of any of the others, very neatly painted and well-furnished, with a nice little verandah in front'. Here, Hunter entertained the tiny English and Portuguese community, along with the odd visiting seamen, at candlelit dinners that represented the ultimate in cultured *farang* social life at the time. But he longed for solid land, and – thanks to his standing at court – received permission to build a substantial brick residence of Western design on the west back, near the Thon Buri end of the present Memorial Bridge. Known to Thais as Hang Huntra, it quickly became a centre for Westerners living in Bangkok and, since there were no respectable hotels, a sort of guest house for notable visitors. Sir John Bowring, for instance, stayed there on his historic mission in 1855, of which more later.

Hunter is also remembered for his part in the career of the famous Siamese twins. The two small boys (actually of Chinese origin) were joined at the chest, but had developed remarkable coordinated skills including swimming, which is what they were doing on the late afternoon when Hunter first saw them while crossing to his house on the Chao Phraya. Later, in partnership with an America sea captain called Abel Coffin, Hunter formed a partnership to send the twins abroad, where they found fame and fortune as an attraction with P. T. Barnum's circus. They never returned to Siam, though they wrote many long letters to Hunter, who read them to the twins' illiterate mother. The two eventually became prosperous farmers in North Carolina, married twin sisters and produced a total of 22 children before their death in 1874. One of their descendants came to Bangkok a few years ago and was interviewed by local papers; a musical based on their life has been produced in Singapore and reportedly has aspirations for Broadway and London. For years, until Anna Leonowens came along, they were the first thing most outsiders thought of in connection with remote, exotic Siam.

Hunter's arrogance eventually led to his downfall. Having already jeopardized relations with the palace by importing opium for sale to local Chinese in open violation of the law, he compounded his difficulties by quarrelling with high-ranking officials and attempting to smuggle sugar, a royal monopoly, out of the country without paying duty. He was finally expelled in 1844 and died four years later in Scotland. His Thai wife, who was half-Portuguese, remained in Bangkok, as did their eldest son Robert, who became an official interpreter during the next reign. 'I regret to say, however,' Dr Bradley commented, 'that like his father he imbibed too frequently and freely of alcoholic spirits. He died suddenly one night in 1865, after a drunken spree of many days duration. My understanding is that he fell off his dock and died of drowning, as so many do in Bangkok.'

Like all of the early Chakri kings, Rama III was a devout Buddhist and a prodigious builder of temples. He was responsible for several of Bangkok's most celebrated present-day landmarks, among them the spectacular *prang*, or Khmer-style tower, at Wat Arun, the Temple of Dawn. An Ayutthaya-period temple, this had served as the royal chapel during King Taksin's reign – the Emerald Buddha had been enshrined there when it was brought back from Laos – and it became a favourite of Chakri rulers. The central tower, 81 m high, surrounded by four smaller ones, was started in the second reign, but – due to the technical problems of building such an immense structure on wet soil – it was not completed until the following one.

The five towers are lavishly adorned with countless pieces of multi-coloured porcelain set in stucco, a decorative touch that

Wat Arun.

delights some outsiders though not all. Geoffrey Gorer, who liked very little of what he saw in Bangkok, was one of the latter. 'The farther away it is seen, the better it looks,' he read in a guidebook. To which he added sourly, 'Yes, indeed. You can't be too far away from these buildings to get the best effect.' Such opinions notwithstanding, the sheer size and elegant shape of Wat Arun are undeniably impressive, and when photography came to Siam not long after the building had been completed, it became perhaps the most famous postcard image of Bangkok. The upper terraces also became a favourite spot from which to take panoramic views of the river and city.

Another temple that received attention from Rama III was Wat Phra Chetupon, popularly known as Wat Po. The largest in Bangkok, it is also the oldest, having been established in the sixteenth century, though almost nothing of its original structures remains. Rama I made extensive renovations, but it was

Rama III who was responsible for most of its best-known features.

One was the huge Reclining Buddha, 46 m long and 15 m high, representing the Buddha at the moment of entering Nirvana. Size more than anything else is what makes this a popular tourist attraction, but the inlaid mother-of-pearl designs on the soles of the feet are masterpieces of an art form that was one of the glories of early Bangkok.

An aspect of Wat Po that goes mostly unnoticed by visitors today is the fact that Rama III attempted to turn it into a sort of open university with a wide range of educational displays. Stone statues that came as ballast on junks returning from the rice trade in China are scattered about, introducing Thais to such animals as the camel, and artificial hills are composed of stones collected from all parts of the kingdom. Murals, stone inscriptions and statuary offer information on astrology, geography, yoga and herbal medicine; a school of traditional massage still flourishes in an eastern corner of the temple.

Of all of Bangkok's many temples, Wat Po is my favourite for a haphazard stroll whenever I happen to be in that part of the city. Some sort of repair work always seems to be going on, as it is at most temples, but Wat Po's vast size defeats wholesale renovation. It usually looks slightly shabby and seldom has the aggressive glitter of, say, the Temple of the Emerald Buddha. You can wander into almost deserted courtyards with nothing but a few monks and perhaps a stray cat or two, picturesquely posed among crumbling monuments; then a step through an ornate gateway, guarded by two towering Chinese demons, brings you to a more lively scene, perhaps a ceremony of some sort, or a class of students sketching some architectural detail. The place reminds me of an attic in a large, old house, not often visited by the tenants; you are always coming across something forgotten or something that you have never noticed before.

Education was also on Rama III's mind at another temple, Wat Yannawa, which is located on the river near the present

Taksin Bridge. This was and remains a very Chinese area, which is no doubt why Rama selected it for a building in the shape of a junk, to remind future generations (so he is supposed to have said) of the vessel that played such an important part in Bangkok's growth and that, even then, was being rapidly replaced by new, faster steamships.

Rama III died in 1851 and was succeeded by his half-brother, Prince Mongkut, but before examining Mongkut's momentous rule it may be worth pausing to take a look at mid-nineteenth-century Bangkok.

Despite the Western-style houses of a few businessmen and missionaries, as well as the Chinese flavour that was then beginning to spread rapidly, it was still, in most regards, an outwardly Thai city, not very different from old Ayutthaya. From Rattanakosin Island, the walled heart, it straggled for some miles downstream along the Chao Phraya, largely on the east bank. Chinatown was already a complex warren of narrow, congested streets and endless activity, and it was steadily expanding southward with its row shops and noisy markets. There were still very few streets. Some 90 per cent of the people lived in what F. A. Neale described as 'a long double, and in some parts treble, row of neatly and tastefully painted wooden cabins, floating on thick bamboo rafts'.

Each floating house was typically three bays deep, the front facing the river and equipped with moveable panels; a water-side veranda served as a bathing area in the morning and evening and as a shop during the day; while the middle bay was for sleeping and the one near land for cooking. The houses were fastened by chains to huge poles driven into the river bed and could thus be easily moved. 'If the air of the "Fleet Street" of Siam does not agree with Mrs. Y and her children,' wrote Neale,

Reclining Buddha at Wat Po.

or they wish to obtain a more aristocratic footing by being domiciled higher up and nearer to the King's palace, then all they have to do is to wait until the tide serves, and loosening from their moorings, float gently up towards the spot they wish to occupy.

The west bank was less populous. Most (though by no means all) of the resident foreigners lived there together with some of the more prosperous Chinese, close to the wharfs, godowns, sawmills and rice mills with which they were making their fortunes. There was a Catholic church, a Protestant mission compound and a few imposing residences like that of the recently departed Robert Hunter, now being used as an official guest house. No bridge spanned the Chao Phraya, which, along with the canals, served as the city's only sewage system; every morning, for example, a small army of royal servants walked out of the palace bearing chamber pots, which they proceeded to solemnly empty into the river.

Bangkok's location spared it severe tropical storms, but it was subject to annual flooding at the end of the rainy season, when water rushing down from the north met high tides from the gulf. At such times, the Sea of Mud became a huge lake, and even Chinatown and the palace area occasionally flooded; but since nobody lived in the Sea of Mud at the time and most houses were raised off the ground to avoid just such a problem, no great damage resulted.

Fires were much more serious, since the city largely consisted of wooden structures. Whipped by wind, a small blaze started by a cooking stove could quickly become a conflagration, and whole neighbourhoods disappeared overnight. Traditional Thai houses were relatively simple structures, however, consisting of prefabricated parts hung on a framework of stout columns, so neighbourhoods reappeared almost immediately, looking much the same.

The most serious threat of all was cholera, which came from India and made its first appearance in the far south at the town of Nakhon Sri Thammarat. It reached Pak Nam, at the mouth of the Chao Phraya, in 1819, probably aboard a ship, and spread from there to the capital. The disease was viewed with superstitious horror, as is suggested by a passage in the Royal Almanac: 'On the 7th month, the waxing moon, a little past 9 o'clock in the evening, a shining light was seen in the northwest and multitudes of people purged, vomited, and died.' Some association of the pestilence with water was recognized, and the royal court had a supply brought from Phetchaburi, 80 km away, where it was collected from a clear stream. For the general public, however, the Chao Phraya was Bangkok's only water supply, and the disease was an annual scourge between April and July, when the river was lowest. One of the worst years was 1849, when between fifteen and twenty thousand died in a single month. At Wat Saket, where the poor could be cremated at government expense, bodies piled up so rapidly they were left exposed to pariah dogs and vultures. The *farang* community suffered equally, according to Dr Malcolm Smith, a British physician who came early in the following century:

The European treatment with astringents, opium, and alcohol was not much better than that used by us in the Middle Ages. It was no more successful than the treatment given by the native doctors whom we despised . . . In those days death claimed its victims swiftly; one evening you sat with your friend, and the next evening you went to his funeral. In the heat of the tropics, the dead do not keep nicely.

Another more pleasant phenomenon, commented on by many early visitors, was what Dr Bradley called 'the far-famed fireflies of the Menam' after nightfall. 'They were playing on the trees that lined the banks of the river,' he wrote.

There was an unbroken chain of them for some ten rods, all flashing their phosphorescence in concert about sixty times a minute. Every flash somewhat resembled a flash of lightning, except that the light was spangled with innumerable bright spots, from which the light emanated. At length, one part of the chain lost its time, then another part, until they had broken into some three or four companies harmonising in their own groups but not as a whole band.

For some reason, fireflies are seldom seen on the Chao Phraya today and never in the dazzling profusion described by Bradley and others. One older resident of Bangkok, who remembers seeing them in his youth, thinks that they were attracted by a particular kind of shrub that once grew profusely along the river, but which has been killed off by the increasing salinity of the water; in support of this theory, he claims to have planted some surviving specimens in his garden and to have been rewarded with at least a modest display.

Rama IV, more usually referred to as King Mongkut, is probably the Chakri ruler best known to the average Westerner. This is not, however, because of his many remarkable qualities as a person, or because of the significant effect he had on his kingdom and on Bangkok in particular. His fame rests largely, and most unfortunately, on the portrait of him drawn in Margaret Landon's *Anna and the King of Siam* and, even more, in *The King and I*, the musical comedy based on it. Both of these were loosely drawn from the memoirs of Anna Leonowens, who was hired to teach some of Mongkut's children. Thais have long been angered by this injustice, for it has resulted in a widely held belief that he was a somewhat comic semi-barbarian who kept a harem and learned the rudiments of civilized behaviour from a virtuous schoolmarm.

In truth, Mongkut developed an extraordinarily broad view long before he ascended the throne. Though he spent his youth in the palace and received the early training of a typical prince, he entered the Buddhist priesthood at the age of 21 and remained a monk for 27 years. During this time, he travelled extensively throughout the country, visiting such ancient capitals as Sukhothai and Ayutthaya and meeting a wide variety of ordinary Thais who talked to him frankly and openly about their life. He also met foreign residents of Bangkok, people like Bishop Pallegoix, Dr Bradley and other missionaries, from whom he learned Latin, French and English, becoming the first royal Thai to speak these languages with any fluency. (Though tolerant of Christianity and appreciative of the missionaries' efforts in medicine and education, he remained sceptical of other aspects; he is supposed to have told one of them, 'What you teach them to *do* is admirable, but what you teach them to *believe* is foolish.') In addition, he developed a lifelong passion for Western science and technology and a determination to bring these new ideas to his country.

Through such exposure, Mongkut was well aware of events outside Siam and of the fact that foreign powers were becoming increasingly interested in the kingdom. The British, he knew, were justifying their occupation of upper Burma at least partly on the grounds that its government persevered in its medieval customs. Thus, as he saw it, the only course was for Siam to modernize, and as quickly as possible.

Two other British emissaries had come to Bangkok after Crawfurd. The first, Henry Burney, had been moderately successful, but the second, Sir James Brooke, the famous 'White Rajah of Sarawak', had been a resounding failure. Clearly, a new initiative was called for, and it came in 1855 with the appointment of Sir John Bowring as Minister Plenipotentiary to China, accredited to Japan, Siam, Cochin China and Korea.

Bowring, who was governor of Hong Kong, was the right man for the job: perceptive, diplomatic and, while not unwilling to exert a little pressure when he felt it was called for, singularly free of most of the prejudices common to Westerners of his time. He read all of the published material on the country and corresponded with Mongkut before he arrived, preparing himself so thoroughly that, although he spent barely a month in Bangkok, he later produced a remarkable two-volume work entitled *The Kingdom and People of Siam* (1857).

Bowring appreciated the Thai talent for pomp and ceremony, beginning with the state barges sent down the river to escort him to the capital. 'Mine was magnificent,' he wrote. 'It had the gilded and emblazoned image of an idol at its prow, with two flags like vanes grandly ornamented. Near the stern was a carpeted divan, with scarlet and gold curtains. The boat was also richly gilded and had a tail like a fish.' And of a later affair at the palace:

> How can I describe the barbaric grandeur, the parade, the show, the glitter, the real magnificence, the profuse decorations of today's Royal audience! . . . On entering the hall, we found it crowded with nobles, all prostrate, with their faces bent to the ground. I walked forward through the centre of the hall to a cushion provided for me in a line with the very highest nobles not of royal blood: the prime minister and his brother were close to me on my right hand. The King came in and seated himself on an elevated and gorgeous throne like the curtained box of a theatre. He was clad in golden garments, his crown at his side; but he wore on his head a cap decorated with large diamonds, and enormous diamond rings were on his fingers.

Away from all the ceremonial glitter, Mongkut and Bowring quickly established a rapport. Mongkut received the envoy in his private apartments at late-night sessions (a custom established by the earliest Chakri kings because of the heat and continued even into the air-conditioned present). There, surrounded by 'beautiful pendules and watches, statues of Queen Victoria and Albert, handsome barometers, thermometers, etc.', as well, sometimes, as a royal child or two, who 'seemed to wear nothing except wide-brimmed hats', the two men talked about a wide variety of subjects.

Bowring occasionally permitted himself a doubt as to whether anything was actually getting achieved, but he persevered, and in time a pioneering treaty was produced that was to have a dramatic effect on Siam's fortunes. Replacing the old policy of export and import monopolies with virtually free trade, it opened Bangkok to world commerce and served as the model for similar treaties with other countries.

Another result was a Thai diplomatic mission to London, whose members were granted an audience with Queen Victoria. On their return, they submitted a report which said in part,

> One cannot help but be struck with the aspect of the august Queen of England, or fail to observe that she must be of pure descent from a race of godly and warlike kings and rulers of the earth, in that her eyes, complexion, and above all her bearing, are those of a beautiful and majestic white elephant.

They could have offered no higher praise. Modern as he was in many ways, Mongkut was a fervent believer in the mystic power associated with these rare creatures, of which he had several pampered specimens in the royal stables. When one of them later died, he sent Bowring a portion of its skin 'with beautiful body-hairs preserved in spirits'; Bowring, in the spirit of science, gave it to the museum of the Zoological Society of London.

Mongkut was also a keen advocate of education, particularly in Western languages. While he sometimes quarrelled with the American missionaries on the subject of polygamy, which they regarded with undisguised horror, he was generally on good terms with most of them and asked three of their wives (among them Mrs Bradley) to teach English to ladies of the Inner Palace. The experiment was not a great success. The women insisted on using Christian tracts, which angered the King and caused him to terminate the classes after a few years. (The royal ladies, it should be noted, were none too keen on the lessons, and most of them dropped out once the novelty wore off.) Mongkut then applied for help to his Singapore agent who – fatefully, one is tempted to say – recommended a widow then struggling to earn her living as a teacher in the British colony.

This is no place for a complete discussion of Anna Harriette Leonowens, but any portrait of Bangkok, indeed of Thailand in general, must consider her, if only because of the prominent position she occupies in the popular non-Thai imagination. Those wishing a fuller account can consult *Louis and the King of Siam*, a biography of her son by Dr W. S. Bristowe, or several articles about her by an American academic, Susan Fuller Kepner. What they should *not* consult, at least for the truth, is Margaret Landon's *Anna and the King of Siam*, *The King and I* or any of the films based on these sources.

Briefly, then, Leonowens was not the well-born Victorian lady legend asserts, but the daughter of a lowly soldier serving in India and a mother who, very likely, was wholly or partly Indian. Her late husband was not a dashing young officer, but a clerk named Thomas Leon Owens, who was the manager of a Penang hotel when he died of apoplexy. Of Leonowens's four children, two had died and one, a daughter, had been sent abroad; only a young son, Louis, remained at the time she received her offer from the King of Siam.

Given the fierce prejudices not only against suspected half-castes but also against people like Thomas Leon Owens in British colonial society – as strong in Singapore as in India – it is no wonder that Anna was eager to put her past behind her, to embark on a new identity as well as a new job, when she sailed for Bangkok in 1862. The deception may not have been deliberate, at least at first; it may have been something that simply happened, over time, in a remote place where, most likely, not too many questions were asked about origins. If so, she was probably not the first, and certainly not the last, Westerner to reinvent herself in the tolerant atmosphere of Siam.

Anna's introduction to Bangkok was unfortunate. She arrived late in the afternoon, no housing arrangements had been made, and she, her small son and two Indian servants were forced to spend their first night aboard the ship that brought them. 'The situation was as Oriental as the scene,' she wrote, in a passage that reveals her prose style as well as the note of barely suppressed hysteria that runs through her work,

> heartless, arbitrary insolence on the part of my employers, homelessness, forlornness, helplessness, mortification, indignation on mine . . . My tears fell thick and fast and, weary and despairing, I closed my eyes and tried to shut out heaven and earth; but the reflection would return to mock and goad me that, by my own act, I had placed myself in this position.

She stayed in Bangkok for five years. Except for a few passages in Dr Bradley's journals and a mention in a letter written by Mongkut's secretary to the Siamese vice consul in Singapore (in which he describes her as 'naughty' and 'very audacious'), the only account of her life there is her own. It was certainly a novel experience, as she would recognize later, and one she could profit from, but it must have been difficult.

Bangkok's expatriate society at the time consisted of four distinct groups who did not often overlap. There was a small diplomatic community, who mostly entertained each other; a handful of missionaries, occupied with good works and prose-lytizing; a few traders of questionable background; and a shifting population of seamen, who stayed for varying lengths of time and were, on the whole, a rough group. For whatever reason, Anna cast her lot with the missionaries. Dr Bradley became a particularly good friend. She supported him in a lawsuit filed against the *Bangkok Recorder* by the French minister (she may, indeed, have supplied the information that caused the minister to sue) and kept in touch with him for a time after she left Siam. Bradley, for his part, considered her to be a 'Christian lady' and sympathized with her many complaints, though he later noted, 'I could have wished that she had appeared more frequently at church on Sunday.' As the only foreign woman regularly in the palace, she must have made some sort of an impression on her students, who included the future King Chulalongkorn. There is no evidence, however, that she influenced King Mongkut in any significant way or that she loomed very large in his life.

Anna left Bangkok in 1867, the year before Mongkut's death, settling first in America and eventually in Canada, where her daughter Avis was then living. In 1870, Dr Bradley received a letter from her in Staten Island saying that she had written some articles about her Siamese experiences for the *Atlantic* magazine. She did not seem nostalgic for her exciting life; instead, she commented, 'Bangkok is the most hideous word I have ever written or uttered.' The articles became a book entitled *The English Governess at the Siamese Court* (1870), which brought Anna considerable acclaim, lecture offers and some much-needed money. She followed it up three years later with *Romance of a Harem* (later reissued as *Siamese Harem Life*), which was less successful. In both books, especially the second, the author (or, conceivably, a ghost writer) embroidered her story with all sorts of lurid additions, including several instances of bald plagiarism. Later, when historians took up the task, it proved a simple matter to utterly destroy her credibility, merely by comparing her account with others of the same period.

By that time, though, few outside Thailand really cared, for Anna Leonowens had become a legend too good to be discarded. Her memoirs, long forgotten and out of print, had been rediscovered in the 1930s by an American missionary named Margaret Landon, posted with her husband to southern Thailand, and in 1944 she had combined them into a best-selling novel called *Anna and the King of Siam*. This was perfect escapist fare amid the grim realities of wartime, and few, if any, bothered about the book's historical accuracy; the author coyly (and misleadingly) asserted that it was '75 per cent fact and 25 per cent fiction'.

Margaret Landon herself would make an interesting subject for a biography (indeed, Susan Kepner has announced that she is working on one). Those who knew her later in Washington,

DC, where her husband became a valued advisor to the US State Department, describe her as a rather stately, strawberry-blonde beauty who bore an uncommon resemblance to some of the actresses who have portrayed Anna on stage and screen. Consciously or not, she may have come to identify herself with her heroine and then gone on to imagine what she herself would have done in similar circumstances, so novel and potentially dramatic. With little to go on beyond a few vague notes Anna had provided in old age for her daughter, perhaps by then half-believing them herself, Mrs Landon fashioned a romantic early life and a much more eventful and influential role in the royal palace. She and her husband were by no means innocents; she must have known that much of what she wrote was nonsense, or at least in sharp contrast to the historical record. Perhaps she kept shifting that 75–25-per-cent ratio and become too absorbed in her fantasies to feel that it mattered.

In any event, it was her book and not Anna Leonowens's that led to the first film version (with Rex Harrison portraying a suave King Mongkut) and then to the famous musical. It was such a good story, so heartwarming; it *ought* to have been true, even though it wasn't.

Mongkut's influence on Bangkok was considerable. Noting the state of most of the city's waterways, for instance, he issued a proclamation advising that

> under no circumstances whatsoever should any person allow himself to throw a dead dog, a dead cat, or the carcass of any other species of animal into any river or canal, whether big or small . . . By the exercise of a little thoughtfulness it should not be too difficult to perceive that other people using the water along the waterway do object to such exhibitions. Were provincial priests from the Lao country and other northern districts or other country gentry to pay a visit to the Divine City and find the said objectionable custom still in practice, they would undoubtedly carry away

the impression that conditions inside the City are not as healthy as outside it, the water supply in the City being so unclean as to breed in the dwellers thereof a number of unhappy ailments. The same or similar impression would be given to Englishmen, Chinese, and all foreign Orientals who come to do business in the Divine City.

From now on should any person disregard His Majesty's gracious advice and still allow himself to practice the said inelegant habits as heretofore, he shall, after due testimony being given against him by his neighbours, be conducted in ignominy around the City by the [governor] as a sorry object of warning to others against committing such an inhuman and irresponsible act of water pollution.

Dry land, too, received his attention. According to Prince Chula's history of the dynasty,

Western people had been accustomed for their health to take the air of an evening riding in horse-drawn carriages, and owing to the lack of suitable roads in Bangkok, they were suffering from bad health and illnesses. [Mongkut] said he was grateful for their complaints, and added that he felt ashamed of the dirt and filth of the narrow lanes of Bangkok, and he began a road and bridge building programme.

Charoen Krung, or New Road as it was known to foreigners, is usually described as the first proper Bangkok street, though actually it was preceded by what is now called Rama IV Road. In 1856 a group of Western merchants proposed that a trading community be established for them some distance from the city, near the present-day Phra Khanong, with a canal leading to the area. Klong Hua Lampong was accordingly dug and the excavated soil piled up along its north bank to make a road. The merchants, however, then refused to move on the grounds that it was too far from Bangkok. New Road was built in 1861, using earth from a canal dug to link Bang Rak and Hua

A view of the New Road.

Lampong canals; it ran parallel to the river for a considerable distance and soon became the principal centre of *farang* trade. When I first came to Bangkok, I lived in Rama IV Road. It was then lined by two canals, neither of them still deep enough for water travel and so regularly used for dumping dead animals that I often thought longingly of Mongkut's punishment for offenders.

Mongkut should also perhaps be given credit for Phu Khao Thong, the Golden Mount, which was long one of Bangkok's most notable sights. It was actually Rama II who first conceived the idea of creating an artificial mountain in the otherwise flat city, but, as with the Temple of Dawn, the mass of mortar and rocks kept stubbornly sinking into the marshy earth. Mongkut returned to the task, using more modern techniques, though the job was not actually completed until the next reign. The result, crowned with a golden spire, remained for many years the highest point in flat Bangkok, visible from almost everywhere and a great favourite with local and visiting photographers. It is still the focus of an annual fair, when hundreds of people climb its winding steps with lighted torches.

The most dramatic changes came as a direct result of the Bowring Treaty. In 1855, the year of his arrival, the envoy noted that 'all that remained to represent foreign trade was one English (half-caste) merchant and a few Anglo-Indians from Bombay and Surat.' Only two years later, some two hundred foreign ships called at Bangkok, and the number increased rapidly thereafter. Rice became a major export for the first time, especially to British India, along with other commodities, such as teak from the north and sugarcane. Embassies and trading companies followed, and soon the city had a sizeable population of Europeans, most of whom lived and worked on or near the river.

Western-style buildings became more common. Most were similar to those seen in British tropical colonies, but some displayed more imaginative touches. Alexander Griswold, one of King Mongkut's biographers, has said that the King liked to adapt European architecture to Siamese needs and that he had a preference for

> cool stuccoed buildings of one storey, ridge-roofed and colonnaded, whose aspect recalled in simpler form the glories of the late Greek Revival in South Carolina and Louisiana – but with judicious touches of the Chinese decoration that had been popular in the previous reign. The combination was harmonious and suitable – and not so bizarre as it sounds, for the formula is basically the same as Chippendale's.

Such structures, among them what appears to have been a replica of London's Big Ben with clocks on each side, rose in the Grand Palace enclosure, side by side with the classic Thai creations of Rama I and the Chinese pagodas and moon gates favoured by Rama III. Most of them were torn down during a far more ambitious building programme in the next reign.

In addition, Mongkut built five new Buddhist temples in the capital and restored twenty others. He also added a new royal barge to the fleet, perhaps the most beautiful of all, an immensely long and slender craft adorned with a seven-headed Naga, or sacred serpent. Processions on the river were common during his reign, some involving hundreds of glittering barges rowed by chanting oarsmen.

The first photographic images of Bangkok also date from this period. Among the pioneers was an Englishman named John Thomson, who arrived from Singapore in the autumn of 1865 and soon afterward applied through the British consul to photograph the royal palace. This request was granted; moreover, the King, deeply interested in the new invention, agreed to have his own portrait taken, first in 'a sort of French Field Marshal's uniform' and later in his court robes. In addition, Thomson photographed the six-day ceremony that celebrated the cutting of the future King Chulalongkorn's topknot. One picture from this group, transformed into an engraving, later appeared in Anna Leonowens's first book of memoirs, captioned 'Receiving a Princess'.

In late 1868 Mongkut and a large party that included the governor of Singapore, journeyed to a remote site on the western coast of the Gulf of Thailand to view a total eclipse of the sun, which the King had accurately predicted. While there, he contracted malaria, dying in the Grand Palace on 18 October. 'It was said,' wrote Dr Bradley, who had known him for 33 years, 'that in the very last moments, the King raised his hands to his face in the usual devotional mode and then, dipping his head backward, ceased to breathe. Truly he died as a philosopher.'

Mongkut's harem, which caused so much comment among the Protestant missionaries and provided most of Anna Leonowens's more sensational inventions, was undeniably a large one. As if to make up for time lost in the priesthood (and also to fulfil the Thai ideal of a virile monarchy), he managed to have a total of 81 children by 27 wives, the largest number achieved by any of his dynasty. In keeping with tradition, he designated no heir, but the choice of the Accession Council fell on his eldest son, fifteen-year-old Prince Chulalongkorn. Because of his youth (and because he was also ill with the fever that had killed his father), it was decided to appoint a regent until he reached the age of twenty. Once again, the succession was a peaceful one, and it was to prove a momentous one. Chulalongkorn would reign for 42 years and leave a lasting royal stamp on Bangkok.

At the very beginning, he demonstrated the passion for change and modernization – which essentially meant Westernization – that became the hallmarks of his reign. In 1871, before his official coronation, he became the first Thai ruler to travel out of the kingdom, going first to Singapore and then to Java. He was warmly received by British and Dutch colonial authorities and came back with a host of new ideas, ranging from a conviction that education must be broadened, to a taste for new forms of architecture.

At his coronation, when he finally assumed full power, he announced the end of a practice that had drawn criticism from foreign observers as far back as the French ambassadors in Ayutthaya. He told those who had come to congratulate him:

> The custom of prostration and human worship in Siam is manifestly an oppressive exaction which an inferior must perform to a superior. The act of showing honour by such prostration and worship His Majesty perceives as of no benefit whatsoever to the country . . . His Majesty proposes to substitute in place of crouching and crawling, standing and walking; and instead of prostration on all fours and bowing with palm-joined hands to the ground, a graceful bow of the head.

This decision was a blow to the very heart of traditional Thai attitudes, not only in the royal milieu but in less exalted households as well. To most of his subjects, especially the ladies of the Inner Palace and their attendants, it was simply unthinkable,

King Chulalongkorn.

and, while not openly protesting, they continued in their old ways. Even in today's democratic society, it is rare to see any Thai head above that of the monarch, and if total prostration is no longer common, there is still a good deal of crawling in the presence of royalty.

Chulalongkorn made no move against another controversial royal custom, that of polygamy, however. The well-guarded enclave within the palace, 'The City of Veiled Women' as Anna Leonowens melodramatically (and inaccurately) termed it, continued to thrive, reaching a peak during the fifth reign. According to Prince Chula Chakrapong, Chulalongkorn took 92 wives, three of them half-sisters, and had 77 children by 36 mothers. As these figures indicate, not all of the wives were honoured with royal favour. Only two of the mothers had more than four children, and the great majority had only one; the remainder hardly ever saw the King except at grand audiences. The women were there as symbols of the ruler's semi-divine powers (like any white elephant discovered within the kingdom) or for political reasons (presented by princes of outlying territories); many were not wives at all, but the daughters of high-ranking nobles who wished to receive training in various elegant arts, such as cooking and flower arrangement, and who would go on to make good marriages outside.

Dr Malcolm Smith described the Inner Palace as

> a town complete in itself, a congested network of houses and narrow streets, with gardens, lawns, artificial lakes and shops. It had its own government, its own institutions, its own laws and law-courts. It was a town of women, controlled by women. Men on special work of construction or repair were admitted, and the doctors when they came to visit the sick. The King's sons could live there until they reached the age of puberty; after that they were sent to stay with relations, or with governors in the provinces. But the only man who lived within its walls was the King.

The population was huge, consisting not only of the present King's wives but also of those of previous reigns, numerous attendants, shopkeepers, speciality cooks, dressmakers and a much-feared female police force known as the *Krom Klone*, who dressed in blue, pantaloon-like garments and white jackets with a cream-coloured scarf across the breast. Anna Leonowens claimed that there were nine thousand residents of the Inner

Palace at the time she taught there. Dr Smith is probably closer to the truth with an estimate of three thousand, but even that is impressive for a relatively small area.

Even today, though the women have long vanished, the Inside is forbidden territory to most visitors. When I did a book on the Grand Palace some years ago, I was given permission to go there with a Thai photographer and walked through its silent streets, still lined with shuttered shops and palaces of often whimsical design in varying states of disrepair. The pleasure gardens were overgrown in places, but their outlines were clear, and a little waterfall still spilled down an artificial hill near a platform where top-knot-cutting ceremonies were held. The photographer was ill at ease even being in such a place and was visibly relieved when the work was finished and we passed back through the tall gates, which closed theatrically behind us.

In countless other matters, Chulalongkorn's changes were successful and, for their day, revolutionary. He abolished slavery, established schools and hospitals, reorganized the government as well as the military forces, and hired foreign experts to advise in the various ministries (British mostly, but also Belgian, Danish, French, German and American). He made the unprecedented decision to send his sons abroad for their education, again favouring England for the majority, but sending some to Germany, Russia and Denmark. He travelled extensively in his own country and made two further trips abroad, in 1897 and 1907, visiting most of the crowned heads of Europe. His foreign policy consisted of playing off one Western power in the region against another, trying to maintain both sovereignty and territorial integrity; while forced to cede territory to the French in Indo-China and to the British in northern Malaya, he succeeded in preserving the independence of the traditional Siamese heartland.

Perhaps because in order to get what they wanted, the French had been so undiplomatic as to send gunboats up the Chao Phraya and moor them within firing distance of the palace, Britain was generally given preference in trade, and Bangkok social life had a strong British flavour. Young men taking up posts in one of the British-owned firms such as the Bombay Burmah Company or the Hong Kong & Shanghai Bank, were expected to leave their cards with the legation as well as with a list of top businessmen, turning up one corner to indicate that they had called in person. They might then be invited to tea and possibly even dinner if they had the right connections. Poor Anna Leonowens would not have survived long in such an atmosphere.

Nowhere was Chulalongkorn's sweeping influence more evident than in Bangkok. A visitor like Carl Bock, who came in 1882, could still enthuse about such exotic sights as 'a sort of aquatic Covent Garden' on the Chao Phraya,

> where dozens of small skiffs are flitting about 'manned' by one or two women, always in tight-fitting white jackets, whose faces are barely seen beneath the broad-brimmed hats of palm-leaves or straw, but whose voices are resonant in all directions, bargaining with their customers, and disposing of their fruit and vegetables, their firewood, and varied upcountry products.

But the British, American, French and Portuguese legations were already very visible structures on the river's east bank, a social club called the Concordia had opened nearby, and a new generation of traders was taking up residence in the capital.

One of these was none other than Leonowens's son Louis, who returned in the early 1880s. The resentment felt over his mother's books does not seem to have attached itself to handsome, hard-drinking Louis, who served Chulalongkorn in various capacities and went on to make a considerable fortune in the teak business in the far north. He established a company named after himself that is still in operation today.

Another trader was a young Danish sailor named H. N. Andersen, who came first in 1872 at the age of 23, and a few years later for a much longer stay. Andersen was placed in command of a royal Thai sailing vessel carrying trade goods from Bangkok to Singapore and Bombay; in 1883 he loaded the holds of the ship with teak, then a somewhat unusual commodity, and took it all the way to Europe, returning with a cargo of coal. This innovative and immensely profitable venture marked the start of his career and eventually led to the founding of the world-wide East Asiatic Company.

While getting his business organized, Andersen lived at a small guest house called the Oriental, run by two fellow Danes on a narrow street leading from New Road to the river. In 1878, it described itself in a new publication called the *Siam Directory* as offering 'Family Accommodations, American Bar, Billiard Saloon, baths, newspapers kept, boats for hire, table d'hote, breakfast at 9 a.m., tiffin 1 .p.m., dinner 9 p.m.' It was thus obviously a cut above the other establishments in the area that catered to visiting sailors, whose boisterous ways were the subject of so many disapproving comments from missionaries like Dr Bradley.

Perhaps it was this distinction that prompted Andersen to buy the place when he became prosperous, or perhaps, with his shrewd business sense, he recognized that the time was ripe for Bangkok to have a proper, world-class hotel to accommodate the more discriminating travellers who were then starting to come by steamship from Singapore and Hong Kong. In 1886, with a loan of 40,000 silver dollars, he filled in the swampy land next to the hotel and developed a street which became known as Oriental Lane. He then tore down the old hotel and began building a new one on the other side of the road. As architects, he called on one of the several Italian firms that had opened in Bangkok to meet the growing demand for impressive Western-style buildings with a classical touch.

The result was unveiled at a grand reception on 14 May 1887, barely a year later, which seems to have been attended by the entire foreign community as well as many aristocratic Thais. Most arrived by boat and strolled across a lawn leading to the

East Asiatic Company building.

hotel's entrance. Staircases led to turrets atop the two wings, from which guests were offered sweeping views of the river that were impossible to enjoy except from the upper levels of such places as the Temple of Dawn and the Golden Mount. Inside, there were Brussels carpets, divans upholstered in peacock-blue velvet, mahogany furniture, 40 guest rooms and a banquet prepared by a chef called Georges Troisouefs, formerly of the French legation.

It was an evening to remember, and the new Oriental's reputation as a centre of Bangkok social life was sealed later that same month with a reception held in honour of Queen Victoria's Golden Jubilee. Today, all that remains of the original building is the so-called Author's Wing, and even that was completely restored after a fire in the 1970s. But the Oriental continues to be the favourite of visiting royals and heads of state and to stress its historical pre-eminence.

Some of those who celebrated the hotel's opening arrived by land. Though no-one then or later (certainly not today) ever praised its architecture, New Road was a busy thoroughfare and well on its way to becoming a centre of Western and Chinese business. It was lined with two-storey shop-houses, mostly of basic design, but some with pretensions of greater permanence. (If you look carefully, you can still discern a few of the latter between Oriental Lane and Silom Road.) In 1889 a Dane called Aage Westenholtz established a horse-drawn tramway on New Road, extending for some 6 km and employing three hundred ponies; this was electrified in 1893, ten years before a similar system was to be seen in Copenhagen. By 1901 the tram network covered 20 km, going all the way to Paknam at the mouth of the river. The tram was still in operation when I arrived in 1960, though by then it had become more of a hazard than a transportation aid. The last section was finally closed in 1969.

Chulalongkorn, meanwhile, was in the process of transforming the Grand Palace. Some of the more hallowed classical buildings were retained in their original form, but much of the rest vanished in a short time, replaced by solid, Western-style structures. The building craze extended to the Inner Palace as well. One structure, erected for Queen Sawang Wadhana, grandmother of the present King, had three floors and open courts in the front and rear, while others were graced by spiral staircases, turrets, false chimneys and rooftop decks for enjoying the view and a rare breath of fresh air in that crowded quarter.

The most important addition to the palace compound was the Chakri Maha Prasat, whose construction began in 1876; it was completed in time for the celebration of Bangkok's centenary in 1882. Designed in Neo-classical style by an English architect called John Clunish, it was originally planned as a domed building, wholly European in appearance. Halfway through the work, however, the King was persuaded to replace the domes with three Thai-style spires to make the structure more harmonious with the older traditional buildings that surrounded it. If perhaps not the first, it was at least an

61

outstanding early example of what would become a Thai penchant for mixing local and foreign architectural styles to achieve something quite different from either. Two years later, it was the first palace building to be illuminated by electric light.

Within, almost everything was European. The King and his principal queen, Saowapa, lived in the Chakri Maha Prasat during the latter part of his reign, and many distinguished visitors were entertained there. One of them, in 1888, was Mrs Florence Caddy, who came as a guest on the Duke of Sutherland's yacht. 'The King's chair of state,' she wrote,

> was placed at the center of the long table; his relatives and nobles, mostly wearing costumes of cloth of gold and kinkob brocades, quite a feast of colour, surrounded His Majesty. We three ladies sat facing the King, divided by the Duke of Sutherland and the Portuguese Minister. The guests numbered about sixty in all. The band in an ante-room played delightfully, national Siamese music alternately with

Chakri Maha Prasat.

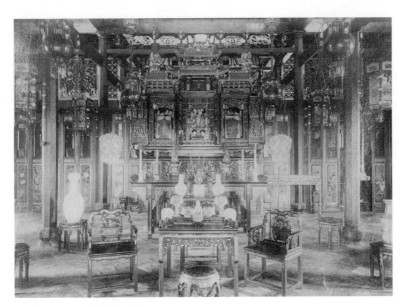

Inside the Grand Palace, 1890s.

selections from 'The Bohemian Girl' and 'Faust,' Valentine's song being especially well-played ... Dinner was served in European style, the glass and porcelain, all from Europe, were engraved and painted with the royal arms and King Chulalongkorn's long name, though perhaps not all his numerous names. The King and princes all drank European wines. The dessert was the only thing presenting any great novelty to us; the sweetmeats were curious, and the fruits various and strange ... After dinner we were conducted into a smaller saloon, richly furnished in the European style. Here the King handed garlands of flowers to many of us, which we hung round our necks or arms. Mine was a chain of alternate white and yellow night scented flowers (yellow the royal colour).

I attended a much larger dinner party in the courtyard of the Chakri Maha Prasat in 1982, one of several events held to celebrate Bangkok's bicentennial. The food was again European, catered, I believe, by the Oriental Hotel, and we too received

63

fragrant garlands of a special sort that had once been fashioned only by ladies of the Inner Palace. A band played Viennese waltzes. After dinner, we went up the double staircase for coffee in the vast reception rooms, hung with portraits of past kings and queens. I remember a wealthy American woman, famous for her jewels, who stood looking out of the tall windows at the illuminated buildings around us. 'My God,' she said, 'It's just like being in *The King and I.*'

One way to get an idea of the changes that were taking place in Bangkok at the turn of the century might be to look at the experiences of Mr and Mrs Émile Jottrand of Belgium, who took up residence in 1898 and kept a journal of their four-year stay. Jottrand had been appointed a legal adviser to the Royal Siamese Government and was thus a newcomer of some importance. While waiting for a house to be made ready, the couple stayed at the Oriental, which had changed hands since Andersen's day and where standards had obviously declined. They were grateful for the hospitality of friends, who asked them to dinner almost every evening: 'Everybody knows the hotel is terrible; they have pity on us and do not want us to eat there, for fear of food poisoning.'

The Jottrands then moved to a temporary home in Bush Lane (named after an Englishman who had served as harbour master in the previous reign), a narrow street leading off New Road to what is now the River City Shopping Centre. This was a slight improvement, despite a detached bathroom and a 'noisy and disagreeable Siamese neighbourhood'. Going for a stroll along New Road, 'the great communication channel', they found frankly appalling. There was

an incessant flow of trishaws, victorias, buggies, etc. without counting the bicycles, the pedestrians, and the tramway which passes at full speed, packed with locals . . . One runs the risk of being rushed off one's feet, squashed, besides being blinded with mud, and having one's clothes dirtied in an instant.

The Jottrands were clearly suffering from what later generations would have called culture shock, a malady that still afflicts many newly arrived *farang* families in Bangkok. Some never recover and leave with horror stories of the modern equivalents of the New Road experience. Others immerse themselves in the place and become a part of the scene. Yet others find an enclave where, surrounded largely by people of their own kind, they manage to live more or less the way they would back home.

The Jottrands chose the third course, or perhaps they had no alternative, eventually moving into a permanent home in one of the new areas that were opening up well away from the river, where 'every house, well separated from the others, is surrounded by a garden which is bordered by a hedge of bindweed, now in blossom'. They had other Belgian neighbours and a smart carriage with a Malay coachman and two little black ponies to carry them about on the rounds of expatriate social life, which seem to have become quite extensive. There were royal receptions at the palace, to which high-ranking foreigners were invited as a matter of course, and meetings with colleagues also employed by the government – Danes advising the army and navy, Englishmen in policing and finance, Belgians in justice, Germans with the railways. In addition, there were evenings at the United Club at the corner of New Road and Siphaya, tea and tennis in the garden of the English legation, festive excursions upriver to the summer palace at Bang Pa-In, and sometimes cultural performances, like one by three ladies from Saigon, which did not find approval from the Jottrands: '. . . third-class singers, old, their voices hoarse, the dress showy, the bosom too well-filled, the décolletage too much in the "hot country" style'.

Dress was a question that concerned them: 'The white costume is very pleasant to wear in this climate, but will the tail coat or a smoking jacket with its starched linen be equally comfortable? It seems that they dance here with spirit, in spite

Bang Pa-In Summer Palace.

of the heat.' Though they hated the hot season and endured a cholera epidemic ('One attends funerals, almost without believing it, for people who twenty-four hours earlier were perfectly well'), the Jottrands appear to have enjoyed their tour of duty. They left with a collection of 'Asian things', some happy memories, a certain sense of accomplishment and, probably, no burning desire to return. (Émile Jottrand was still alive in 1960, when the present King paid a state visit to Belgium.)

Chulalongkorn devoted great attention to the improvement of Bangkok. Dozens of new roads were built, leading away from the river, as well as bridges over the canals. It became a tradition for the King to open a new bridge on his birthday; these were known as Saphan Chalerm (literally 'Birthday Bridges'). Most have disappeared with the canals, but a few survive, including Chalermla, on Phaya Thai Road, popularly known as Saphan Hua Chang, or Elephant's Heads Bridge, because of its triple-headed elephant decorations.

His most concentrated effort at city planning took place in the Dusit district, north-east of the palace, then largely empty except for a few fruit orchards. To reach the area, he built a broad boulevard called Ratchadamnoen ('Royal Progress'), five km long and consisting of three carriageways separated from one another by double rows of trees and bordered by shady sidewalks. According to Prince Chula, this was inspired by the King's first visit to Europe, being 'based partly on the Mall in London and partly on the Champs-Élysées in Paris'. The rest of Dusit also resembles a well-planned European city, with wide, tree-lined avenues, a zoological garden and stately buildings set in large compounds, as well as a palace where the King planned to reside, and a new temple, Wat Benchamabopit, constructed mainly of Italian marble. 'Immediately the new site [of the palace] was selected,' wrote one contemporary, 'a veritable land boom took place in the surrounding district, and the clearing of the jungle and the filling in of the swamp took place with astounding rapidity for Siam. Roads were planned in all directions and buildings sprang up like mushrooms.'

All of this is still very clear today, but Dusit, alas, was not to become the model for a new and better Bangkok. The King did not live to see the completion of his new palace, though he did enjoy the comfort of several others in the area, including Vimarn Mek ('Celestial Residence'), a spectacular golden-teak creation with 81 rooms. Near Wat Benchamabopit is Chitrlada Palace, originally a country villa and the residence of the present King. Most of the other buildings in the district are now used as offices for the government and the military, and the pavements are largely empty after dark.

This was true barely ten years after Chulalongkorn's death. Driving down the avenues in early 1923, Somerset Maugham thought,

They are handsome, spacious and stately, shaded by trees, the deliberate adornment of a great city devised by a king ambitious to have an imposing seat; but they have no reality. There is something stagy about them, so that you feel they are more apt for court pageants than for the use of every day. No one walks in them. They seem to await ceremonies and processions. They are like the deserted avenues in the park of a fallen monarch.

Other new streets were by no means deserted. Complaints about Bangkok's traffic were common in the early years of the twentieth century and would become a leitmotif in almost all descriptions, rising to a perpetual wail of despair in modern times.

In 1871 a wealthy Chinese presented the first rickshaw to the King, and within a single generation there were so many that, in 1901, the government felt compelled to pass a law limiting their number. Joining them were horse-drawn vehicles of all kinds, from simple gharries to elegant coaches that could transport a whole family, humbler carts pulled by dogs, bicycles and tram cars. The first automobile, driven by one of the King's sons, caused a stir in 1902; six years later, there were three hundred in the city. Within a short time, the water transport that had been so vital to Bangkok's existence became irrelevant to a large part of its population.

The importance of the Chao Phraya and other major waterways had also been reduced. The first railway, constructed by a Belgo-Danish company, was opened in 1893, linking the capital with Paknam, a distance of 25 km. For political and strategic reasons, another to Nakhon Ratchasima, on the edge of the north-eastern plateau, was started by the government in 1892; it reached Ayutthaya, 72 km away, in 1897, and the whole line was completed in 1900. By 1910 there was an eastern line to Chachoengsao on the gulf, a northern line to Uttaradit, and a southern line to Petchaburi, all of which would have been regarded as remote less than a generation before.

An early car rally at Sanam Luang, outside the Grand Palace.

The first guidebook to the country appeared in 1904, written by one J. Antonio, a Portuguese who also operated a photography studio that produced images of early twentieth-century Siam used in many subsequent books. 'Bangkok,' he proclaimed,

> is veritably a city of Hotels, that is to judge by the number of signboards which meet the eye everywhere, but few of these can be recommended. The leading one is the Oriental where extensive improvements and additions have of late been made. The stranger may also be made comfortable at the Hotel de la Paix (better known to Bangkokians as Mme Toni's), the Hotel d'Europe, or the Bristol or Palace Hotels.

Antonio's guide informs his readers that European residents are not confined to one part of the city, but 'pretty evenly scattered throughout the whole' (the same is true today) and offers a surprisingly long list of clubs and associations where they could enjoy their leisure time, among them the British Club, the Royal Bangkok Sports Club, the Bangkok Amateur Dramatic

Society, the Siam Society and the Harmony Club (all but the last are still going strong). A vocabulary section offers the Siamese for a number of words and phrases that might also come in handy today, such as 'Do you speak English?', 'This is too much' and 'This curry is very good'. (There is no longer much use, of course, for 'Pull the punkah, boy' and 'Get me a carriage'.)

King Chulalongkorn died on 23 October 1910, a date still observed as a public holiday. Even at the time, it was recognized as the end of an era, just as Victoria's passing was in England, one in which almost every aspect of society was changed in some way. It had not been quite so traumatic as the Meiji Era in Japan – foreigners and their customs had never been forbidden in Siam – but it had been just as radical in its way, and its effects were perhaps more lasting. Over the years, a sort of Chulalongkorn cult has grown up, especially in Bangkok. Statues and photographs of him are often placed at shrines, both public and private, and large numbers of people, particularly Chinese, gather at his equestrian statue in the Royal Plaza to offer floral wreaths, not only on 23 October but on other occasions as well. The reason for this is somewhat obscure – adherents say only that that they hold him in great respect – but it is evidence of the unique power this monarch wields after nearly a century.

The city that was in place in 1910 is still there for the most part today. Because it would be unseemly, indeed illegal, to look down on the King's residence, no really tall new buildings have gone up in Dusit or near the Grand Palace, and most of the old ones remain, sometimes restored to their former splendour, sometimes quietly rotting away. For different reasons, the same is true of crowded Chinatown and the streets leading in and out of it. There have been more changes along the Chao Phraya, but even so, amid the towering condominiums and hotels of the last few decades, numerous reminders of the fifth reign can be glimpsed.

There is, for example, the immense Bangkhunprom Palace, built by one of Chulalongkorn's sons who was sent to Germany for his education. Now part of the Bank of Thailand, the palace was designed by a German architect in a splendid medley of the assorted styles then in favour among the Thai aristocracy: a bit of Renaissance, a touch of Baroque, a seasoning of Rococo and Art Nouveau. Further down the river and just across from Wat Arun, the Temple of Dawn, is Chakrabongse House, a relatively plain structure with a turret and a widow's walk, built by another son, not as a principal residence but as a place to change into formal dress when going by boat to gatherings at the Grand Palace, just upstream.

Rachini School, founded by Queen Saowapa as the first girls' school operated by Thais, is also there, with the words 'Royal Seminary' on its pediment, as are the Portuguese and French embassies and the old Customs House, where duties were levied on all ships coming to the city. The school and the embassies still perform their original functions, but the Customs House, alas, has been allowed to fall into semi-ruin, occupied by the fire brigade and sternly closed to inquisitive visitors. Next door to the Oriental Hotel, still boasting its original façade, is the gleaming white building that used to be the headquarters of H. N. Andersen's East Asiatic Company.

On the west bank of the river, where development was much slower due to the lack of bridges, the busy sawmills have nearly all gone, but many of the mansions built by wealthy Chinese families can still be seen, along with the enormous old godowns where produce was stored before being shipped abroad. At one point, too, next to the Marriott Royal Garden hotel, quite far from the centre of old Bangkok, there is a nostalgic view of the First Presbyterian Church, built in 1910 on the site of an older one dating from 1860. Full of apprehension, Anna Leonowens saw the earlier building as she sailed into Bangkok and felt that

the gentle swaying of the tall trees over the chapel imparted a promise of safety and peace, as the glamour of the approaching night and the gloom and mystery of the pagan land into which we were penetrating filled with me with an indefinable dread.

Already by the year of Chulalongkorn's death the capital had begun to expand eastward in a tentative way. Siphraya, Suriwong, Silom, and Sathorn roads had been built, linking Rama IV and New Road, with houses and shops along them. Some particularly grand houses stand along Sathorn, which became popular with wealthier Europeans.

At the corner of Rama IV and Henri Dunant roads is Chulalongkorn Hospital, another pet project of Queen Saowapa, who had a keen interest in medical matters (nine times a mother, she was the first of the royal ladies to whole-heartedly embrace modern methods of childbirth and sponsored a school for Thai midwives). On Henri Dunant (named after the founder of the Red Cross) is the oldest part of Chulalongkorn University. This originated in the palace in 1902 as the Royal Pages School to train provincial administrators, then was moved to its present site as the Civil Services College. In 1917 King Rama VI raised it to the status of Siam's first university and named it after his father. Its early buildings display that whimsical blend of Thai and Western architecture that was typical of the era and that today misleads some visitors into thinking that they must be part of some temple. For the better part of 30 years, I worked in one of those buildings. It had open tiled verandas and immensely tall red doors through which storms occasionally swept, scattering students' exam papers. Owls and bats nested in the upper reaches. I never walked into it without being intensely aware that it was a very special place.

Across the street from the university are the rich green golf links and playing fields of the Royal Bangkok Sports Club, established by royal charter in 1901. Though it was primarily conceived by Westerners and run along the lines of a British club, the Sports Club, unlike similar ones in Singapore and

Penang, was never an exclusively *farang* domain. Thais were on the general committee from its inception, and they were free to join providing they had a taste for such Western sports as horse-racing, golf, cricket, squash and tennis. Quite a few of the young men sent abroad for their education by Chulalongkorn did develop such tastes, especially for horse-racing, and the club has always been proud of its royal origins. The membership, however, remained predominately *farang* until the dark days of the Second World War, when it was preemptorily taken over by the Japanese and its British, Dutch and American members marched off to internment camp. After the war, it struggled back to life, regaining its old status as the city's most élite social institution, now with an overwhelmingly Thai membership.

In January 1911, while the country was still mourning the passing of King Chulalongkorn, a large crowd turned out to watch a strange contraption move down the Sports Club's race-track. A French aviator named Charles Van Den Born, in a flimsy-looking Henri Farman biplane, was giving Bangkok its first experience of the new wonder of flight in a heavier-than-air machine, just eight years after it had been introduced by the Wright brothers on a lonely North Carolina beach in America. 'Whether the biplane is an easy machine to handle,' reported the *Bangkok Times*, the leading English-language paper of the day,

> or whether the skill of Mr. Van Den Born makes it appear so is difficult to tell. At any rate the flights accomplished were to all appearances easy and graceful. The quiet manner in which the machine simply drifted off into the air and the smoothness with which the land was regained elicited much admiration.

A number of the spectators, including a Thai princess, were bold enough to pay fifty *baht* for the privilege of going up. What they saw were the few buildings that then housed Chulalongkorn Hospital and the Civil Services College, the racetrack and mostly open fields and gardens around Saladaeng, at the corner of Silom and Rama IV roads, now one of Bangkok's busiest commercial centres. What would become the Royal Thai Air Force was established a few years later, led by pilots who had been sent to France for their training. They continued to use the Sports Club track for some time, storing their planes in hangars on the site of the present Police Headquarters, before they moved out of town to Don Muang, one of the rare flood-free elevations north of the capital. Few of the millions of passengers who pass through today's international airport know that it is one of the oldest in the world still being used in its original location.

While old landmarks remained virtually unaltered, Bangkok continued to change, at a somewhat slower pace, during the next three decades. King Rama VI (Vajiravudh) was the first Thai ruler to receive his education abroad, and, like his father, he was an enthusiastic builder. Among his surviving contributions is the slightly over-the-top Venetian-Gothic edifice near the Marble Temple that now serves as the office of the Prime Minister and another, with vaguely Tudor overtones, that is designated as the official Prime Minister's residence (though none of them have ever actually lived there). Rama VI began construction of Chulalongkorn University and erected a row of large Victorian houses along Ratchadamri Road for lease to some of the foreigners who worked for the government (they are lived in now by American Embassy employees). Towards the end of his reign, in 1925, he also donated the land for Lumpini Park. It was supposed to be the setting for a grand Siamese Kingdom Exhibition, and various facilities – lakes, roads, display halls, a Chinese pagoda, a sports stadium – were already in place when he suddenly died, two months before his 44th birthday. One of his successor's first acts was to cancel the event, though the park remained and would be Bangkok's only such open space for the next 60 years.

Despite his foreign education, or perhaps because of it, Rama VI was a fervent nationalist, determined to raise his kingdom's status in the world and rid it of any lingering suggestions of inferiority. His official coronation a year after Chulalongkorn's death was attended by representatives from Great Britain, France, Russia, Germany, Japan and the US, who were treated to the full splendour of ancient Thai ritual. He expanded education and introduced the novelty of team sports, particularly football, to create a greater sense of unity. Alarmed by the growing economic power of Bangkok's Chinese population – most of whom, even after generations, still regarded China as their home and sent a good deal of their money there – he wrote a series of articles for local newspapers and published a long essay ominously entitled *The Jews of the Orient* (1914). At the outbreak of the First World War, Siam proclaimed its neutrality, but, in 1917, war was declared on the Central Powers and a small expeditionary force was sent to France. They saw little action (the war ended shortly after they arrived), but the political benefits were considerable; Siam signed the Treaty of Versailles and, more importantly, gained vital support from the US in the renegotiation of unequal clauses in international treaties.

In addition, Rama VI gave his country a new national flag and introduced the use of surnames. The old flag, which dated from Rama II's time, showed a white elephant on a red background. To the King, this was not dignified enough for a modern nation; the elephant was sometimes crudely rendered so that it might be mistaken for a pig, and, worse, it was occasionally inadvertently flown upside down. In any event, over some objections, Rama VI decided on a change, and a new design was unveiled in 1917 to coincide with Siam's entry into the World War. It was composed of three stripes – red, white and blue – which, said the literary-minded King, represented the nation, the Buddhist faith and the monarchy.

Surnames, proposed four years earlier, were a more complex and significant innovation. Until that time, most Thais had been known only by their given names, sometimes pure Thai words for fruits, flowers, animals or personal characteristics, sometimes more impressive Sanskrit or Pali words; in a village-oriented world, these were sufficient. Members of the governing élite were known by their titles or ranks; these could change as they rose (or sometimes fell), causing difficulty to outsiders and keepers of historical records.

By the early twentieth century, society had changed to such a great degree that some more reliable system was clearly needed, if only to keep an accurate record of births, deaths, marriages and tax matters, not to mention putting an end to judicial confusion. Two factors were probably uppermost in the King's mind: to show that Thais were the equal of Westerners in such things, and to distinguish between Thais and Chinese, who were still inclined to use clan names.

Under the new law, all Thais had to have a surname, which, in turn, would be handed down through the male line, as in Western countries. Surnames had to be suitable (some were restricted to royalty), and no two families could register the same one. It was an immensely complicated process and time-consuming as well, especially in rural areas; the original deadline had to be set back several times and was still not reached by the end of Rama VI's reign. Gradually, though, compliance was achieved, first in Bangkok (where it is said that the King himself devised more than three thousand names) and then in the countryside.

In one respect, the ideal of emulating the West was not a success. Thais still use the first name more frequently than the last, so that a political leader like Pridi Phanomyong is generally referred to in newspapers and history books simply as Pridi, and among school children even best friends will often not know one another's family names. On the other hand, the use of surnames has certain advantages to an outsider as well as to government record keepers. It helps sometimes to keep track of large families, where it may provide the only apparent link, and it can also help to spot naturalized Chinese, especially recent ones, who tend to have the longest, most intimidating surnames.

Rama VI broke with tradition in other ways as well. He was opposed to polygamy. He refused to marry anyone at all until the very end of his reign, and then produced a single child, a girl, born a day before his death. As a result, the mysterious world of the Inner Palace slowly disintegrated. Most of the women moved out, taking their attendants with them; a few lingered for years in bewildered solitude. Queen Saowapa, highest ranking of them all, who had spent her entire life in the palace (she was a daughter of King Mongkut and thus had married her half-brother) moved to Phya Thai Palace, where, keeping up old habits, she proceeded to turn night into day. She breakfasted at around 6:00 p.m. and held audiences after midnight; men with blow-guns and clay pellets were supposedly employed to keep the noise of birdsong down during the day.

Rama VI probably could never have attracted the sort of passionate devotion his father enjoyed; the shadow was simply too large, the memories too vivid. To the great majority of rural Thais, isolated in their fields and mountains, it mattered little; he was still the Lord of Life, suffused by the ancient magic of monarchy. In Bangkok, however, it was different, and for several reasons. Members of the élite resented the way he surrounded himself with a clique of his own choosing, among them a paramilitary group called the Wild Tigers, and by his reluctance to listen to older members of the royal family, even his mother, who continually (and vainly) proposed suitable young women for marriage. To others, there was the matter of his obvious anti-Chinese stance; a significant part of Bangkok's population by that time was Chinese, some of them second or third generation.

History was against Rama VI, too, in a way. New and ominous forces were stirring across the world. By the early 1920s, two of the monarchies that had sent representatives to his coronation had fallen; Tsar Nicholas of Russia and his family had been murdered by the Communists who overthrew them; talk of revolution seemed to be universal. Rama VI was aware of all this and appeared to be interested in the idea of democracy. At Phya Thai Palace, where he took up residence after Queen Saowapa's death, he built an elaborate miniature city called Dusit Thani, complete with rivers, roads, a railway, a wide range of buildings and its own newspaper. There were two political parties, a constitution, elections for mayor. Whether this was a serious democratic experiment, as some have claimed, or merely fun and games, it is difficult to say; whatever the intent, it led to no significant changes in the absolute monarchy.

Finally, there was the simple fact that the country was encountering severe financial problems, caused partly by the King's lavish spending and partly by poor rice crops and economic slumps abroad. In 1925 the cancelled Siamese Kingdom Exhibition in Lumpini Park was not the only sign that difficult times lay ahead.

In 1922 the British minister made an announcement that profoundly shocked many of his countrymen and that would have important effects on Bangkok's development. The old legation, he said, described by Somerset Maugham as 'trim, green, old-fashioned and dignified', would soon be moving from the riverside to a new site, described by another visitor, with some dismay, as being 'on the fringe of town'.

Actually, there had been talk of moving as early as 1902, to escape the congestion of New Road and non-stop noise from the sawmills on the west bank, but for various reasons no definite steps had been taken. It is said that Sir Robert Greg, who had arrived as minister in 1921, was not in fact in favour of the move; he and his wife liked the old residence and were 'horrified at the thought of being obliged to live in a house designed by an architect from the Ministry of Works whose achievements are widely regarded as architectural monstrosities'.

Design problems were overcome, however, and, in the autumn of 1926, an impressive collection of new buildings in solid colonial style was ready, facing a then largely empty Ploenchit Road. With the legation staff went a bronze statue of

Queen Victoria and a steel flagstaff reputed to be the tallest in South-east Asia. For their old site, now the headquarters of the Post Office, the British received enough money from the Siamese government to buy the new piece of land, erect all the buildings and still have a substantial sum left over.

The land was bought from a Chinese entrepreneur named Lert Sresthaputra, better known as Nai Lert, who owned a trading company in the old part of Bangkok and a ferry-boat service on a canal that had been cut through the eastern suburbs. Nai Lert also wanted relief from the pressures of the crowded city, and since land in the Ploenchit area was cheap and accessible by canal, he bought a considerable amount of it. In the early '20s, he built a large but simple teak house for himself and his family, essentially an airy pavilion raised off the ground, and began spending weekends there, gradually expanding the structure. The family took up full-time residence in 1927, by which time he had the British for neighbours and had also subdivided the rest of his land into building plots and streets, including part of present-day Wireless Road, along which he planted shady rain trees. It was the beginning of a new centre, mainly residential at first, which within a few years was regarded as quite convenient after all. The Nai Lert house, the British Embassy, the streets and many of the original rain trees are still there. Nai Lert's daughter was for a time my landlady and used to tell me stories about coming out to the property for 'country weekends' when she was young and also about the bomb – American, I think – that fell on the house during the war, doing a good deal of damage but miraculously not killing anyone.

Two views of Bangkok in the 1920s may offer some idea of how the city then impressed outsiders.

One from Somerset Maugham, mentioned earlier. With his companion, Gerald Haxton, the already famous writer arrived in the winter of 1923 after a gruelling overland journey through the Shan States of northern Burma. The fact that he was coming down with a bad case of malaria may have influenced his initial jaundiced impressions.

A card that Maugham and Haxton were handed by a street tout suggests that one aspect of Bangkok's later reputation was already well in place. 'Oh, gentleman, sir,' it read in part, 'Miss Pretty Girl welcome you Sultan Turkish Bath, gentle, polite massage, put you in dreamland with perfume soap.' The offer cannot have held much appeal, and not just because of the malaria. Nor did New Road,

> the main artery of the city, five miles long . . . lined with houses, low and sordid, and shops, and the goods they sell, European and Japanese for the most part, look shop-soiled and dingy. A leisurely tram crowded with passengers passes down the whole length of the street, and the conductor never ceases to blow his horn. Gharries and rickshaws go up and down, ringing their bells and motors sounding their claxons. The pavements are crowded and there is a ceaseless clatter of the clogs the people wear. Clopperty-clop they go and it makes a sound as insistent and monotonous as the sawing of the cicadas in the jungle.

Maugham escaped the clamour in the Oriental Hotel, where his fever rose to alarming heights, and it seemed for a time that he might die. (He overheard the German manageress telling his doctor to move him before that happened.) But he gradually improved, and, once able to get about, he discovered more appealing aspects of the city.

The Buddhist temples came as a revelation. Unlike Geoffrey Gorer and some other Westerners (especially those drawn to the spare architecture of Japan), Maugham found the Siamese taste for excess in religious art exhilarating:

> They are unlike anything in the world, so that you are taken aback, and you cannot fit them into the scheme of the things that you know. It makes you laugh with delight to think that anything so fantastic could exist on this sombre earth ... I do not know that these Siamese wats have beauty, which they

say is reserved and aloof and very refined; all I know is that they are strange and gay and odd, their lines are infinitely distinguished, like the lines of a proposition in a schoolboy's Euclid, their colours are flaunting and crude, like the colours of vegetables in the greengrocer's stall at an open-air market, and, like a place where seven ways meet, they open roads down which the imagination can make many a careless and unexpected journey.

He was equally charmed when a friend took him on a tour of the *klongs*. By that stage in Bangkok's development, these were mostly across the river in Thon Buri, as they are today, and then (and now) they offered a welcome contrast to streets like New Road. 'To the unaccustomed eye,' wrote Maugham in a description that still applies to some of the more outlying waterways,

it is surprising to see a decent old woman with a mop of grey hair deftly manoeuvring her canoe amid the traffic as she goes methodically about her day's shopping. And like children scampering across the road, tiny boys and girls, sometimes stark naked and seldom with more than a rag about their loins, dart in and out among the steamers and motor-boats in tiny little dugouts that make you wonder that they are not run down. On the houseboats people lounge about idly; men mostly half-naked wash themselves or their children; and here and there half-a-dozen urchins scramble about in the water.

A different sort of view is provided by Erik Seidenfaden in a 1928 guidebook for the Royal State Railways of Siam, which was aimed at prospective tourists. Seidenfaden painted an alluring panorama that allegedly could be seen from the summit of the Golden Mount:

Along the city moat we see the city wall with its embrasures, and just where the broad Ratchadamnoen Boulevard crosses

81

the moat there still remains one of the old picturesque forts. Looking westward, one can see the tall roofs of Wat Suthat and the top of the red painted swing while further away over a labyrinth of house tops and big administrative buildings are seen the Grand Palace with the glittering spires of Chakri Palace, the Dusit Maha Prasat, and the shimmering fabric of the golden chedi inside Wat Phra Keo. To the south of the palace flash the gilt gables of Wat Po and further away, on the other side of the river, the slender prang of Wat Arun soars upward . . . Looking to the south the horizon is closed as by a mighty forest, the vast and idyllic garden land on the west bank of the river, from which here and there some white prang or pointed chedi peep up out of all the greenery. On this side of the river, towards the south and southeast, the newer part to the capital extends with its throng of streets and houses, presenting a view which however, is not that of a desert of stones like so many American and European cities because here in Bangkok the trees and the verdure dominate. Seen from a high position, the town resembles one huge park, though here and there tall chimneys belonging to rice mills or factories belch forth their smoke indicating that this is really a living and prospering town. Continuing, our eyes travel towards the east where among other buildings we can just discern the tall arched roof of Bangkok's Railway Terminus and furthermost east a glimpse is seen of the red towers of the Phya Thai Palace and then turning to the north we see the tree tops of Dusit Park and the white marble struc-ture of the Throne Hall with its cupola. From the Throne Hall our eyes can now follow the broad and stately avenue of Ratchadamnoen up to its end at the precincts at the Grand Palace.

One suspects that Seidenfaden indulged in a bit of poetic licence, even in 1928, with his insistence on predominant 'trees and verdure'. And he was certainly no seer, as is proven else-where in the book when he confidently predicts, 'The future

will see Bangkok as a vast, well laid out, park-like town, inter-
sected with a network of broad shaded roads running in all
directions.' But on a rare smogless day, nearly all of the landmarks he mentions can still be seen from the Golden Mount,
including Phya Thai Palace, which at the time was serving as a
luxury hotel operated by the government and is now part of the
Phra Mongkut Military Hospital. I had occasion to visit the
former palace, hoping to find traces of the miniature city Rama
VI had built in its gardens for his experiment in democracy.
None remained, but a graceful little audience hall where his
mother used to receive guests is still there, recently restored,
and so is a Romanesque pavilion in the garden where hotel
guests used to be treated to performances of Thai classical
dance by moonlight, a magical experience no doubt.

The next three decades were difficult for Bangkok and the
country as a whole. The Great Depression of the early 1930s
soon reached the kingdom, along with the political turmoil that
accompanied it almost everywhere. The price of rice, on which
the Thai economy depended, fell by two-thirds, and land
values dropped to as little as a sixth of what they had been
before. King Rama VII, who had received scarcely any training
to prepare him for the throne, made an effort to trim government expenditures, but only succeeded in alienating already
hard-pressed civil servants and military officers.

On 24 June 1932, while Rama VII was on holiday at a seaside
palace ironically called 'Far From Care', a small group of
middle-level officials – most of them educated abroad – staged
a *coup d'état*, and without a shot Thailand's centuries-old
absolute monarchy came to an end. Rama VII agreed to remain
under a constitutional government, but relations between him
and the new regime soon deteriorated. In 1934 he went to
England for medical treatment, and the following year he abdi-
cated; Prince Ananda Mahidol, then a ten-year-old student in
Switzerland, was proclaimed the new King by the National
Assembly, but remained abroad with a regent acting for him.

Ananda's reign was to be mostly absent and ended in tragedy; on a visit in 1946, he was shot dead in the Grand Palace, by whom and for what reason it has never been precisely determined. He was succeeded by his younger brother, who still reigns as the much-beloved King Bhumibol Adulyadej and who, in 1996, became the world's longest-ruling monarch.

Despite the slump, Bangkok continued to expand. The first bridge was opened across the Chao Phraya in 1932, just a few months before the end of the absolute monarchy, and Thon Buri became increasingly attractive for settlement. A much more popular area of growth was along Sukhumwit Road, a highway leading to the east coast of the Gulf, deep into the Sea of Mud, meant to protect the city from invasion. The pattern here was similar to that followed by Nai Lert when he opened the Ploenchit area and in others as well. A well-to-do family would acquire a large piece of land, build a house for themselves – often several houses for different members of the family – on one plot and then parcel off the rest for sale. In this way, a complex network of streets developed between Sukhumwit and New Petchburi roads, with Klong Saen Saeb, a major waterway, running through it. Prior to 1950, houses were comparatively sparse, but this area was already becoming known as one of Bangkok's more élite residential areas, especially with a new generation of up-and-coming Chinese and civil servants. Thanks to a growing number of automobiles (mostly imported from England and America) and to an efficient bus system (one of the first was the White Bus Company, owned by the industrious Nai Lert), people were moving out of the polluted, insanitary old city to enjoy the luxury of a proper house set in a garden.

Some of the *sois*, or small streets, off Sukhumwit acquired a distinct flavour. Chitr Phoumisak, a poet with Marxist leanings who was killed by the police in the mid-1960s, wrote a poem called 'Fishiness in the Night' lamenting Bangkok's fame as a sex centre. One line reads, 'Saen Saeb Canal wincing from the madness of lust, suffocating from its fishy smells.' Thai readers, at least some of them, would have understood the allusions here. The name of the canal literally means 'one hundred thousand stings', a reference to the mosquitoes that swarmed around it, but the canal was also notorious for its floating brothels, and one of the city's most élite red-light districts was on Soi Klang, which led to it. (No longer. The floating brothels, each holding a girl in a curtained pavilion, disappeared around the time Chitr Phoumisak was murdered, and Soi Klang, now more prosaically called Soi 49 – I live just off it – is a staid street of houses, hospitals and apartment buildings.)

Thus, following a pattern established in old Bangkok, Sukhumwit never became purely residential. Indeed, no part of the city is, with the possible exception of a few 'housing estates' that have walls around them and guards at their entrances. The grandest millionaire's mansion, with gilded gates and a vaguely Roman façade, may have an open-fronted noodle shop next door, and next to that a private hospital. Older houses are constantly being transformed into restaurants; once, I went to dinner at a new Italian place and only after some time realized that I was sitting in the bedroom of someone I knew twenty years ago.

Several other distinctive landmarks were added in the 1920s and '30s. Italian architects, painters and sculptors flocked to Bangkok in the last years of King Chulalongkorn's reign to design and decorate everything from palaces to bridges. One of the last to arrive was Corrado Feroci, invited by King Rama VI to produce a collection of bronze statues celebrating the exploits of past Thai heroes. This he did, in addition to creating the statue of Rama VI which stands at the entrance to Lumpini Park; in fact, he stayed on, married a Thai woman, founded Silpakorn (Fine Arts) University, and eventually took the Thai name of Silpa Bhirasri. Feroci seems to have had no problem adjusting to the new order. He designed both the Democracy Monument in the middle of Ratchadamnoen Avenue (1939) and, two years later, the even larger and more elaborate Victory Monument to commemorate the successful outcome of a brief

The Democracy Monument.

war against the French of Indo-China, as a result of which the lost territories in Laos and Cambodia were regained. (Only for a short time; they had to be returned at the end of the war.)

One writer has described these two monuments as being 'in the mode of Heroic Realism of the type popular in Germany and Italy at the time'. To some, they may seem equally akin to those massive edifices so loved in Stalinist Russia, adorned with muscular, determined, stern-faced figures that convey little suggestion of the small, graceful people who pass them every day. Also from the same period (but not designed by Feroci) are the severe buildings that line the upper part of Ratchadamnoen Avenue. These must, at the time of their construction, have seemed the latest in ultra-modern city architecture, at least of the type seen at world fairs. Today, they look stained, shoddy and graceless, a far cry from the elegant boulevard envisioned by Chulalongkorn after his visits to Paris and Berlin.

Bangkok was spared serious damage during the Second World War. Under an authoritarian government led by Field Marshal Pibulsonggram (more commonly known merely as Pibul), the country's name was changed to Muang Thai, or Thailand, in 1939, reflecting a nationalistic tendency to stress the primacy of the Thais above other inhabitants (particularly the Chinese). Another, rather more curious, aspect of Pibul's program was a series of 'cultural mandates' which urged Thais to adopt such Western fashions as hats for women and shirts and shoes for men; people who failed to comply were refused service in government offices. These novelties were more or less laughed out of existence after a year or so, but some of them had a lingering effect; when I first arrived in the city in 1959, taxi drivers were technically required by law to wear a hat, which they usually hung over the rear-view mirror.

The country's leaders paid close attention to the war in Europe and came to the justifiable conclusion that British pledges to aid in their defence were unrealistic. Thus they strengthened ties with increasingly belligerent Japan and acquiesced to its request to pass through Thai territory when the invasion of Malaya commenced on the morning of 8 December 1941. In fact, Pibul was conveniently out of town, where exactly nobody seemed to know, when the request was made; the Japanese went ahead with their plans anyway.

Thailand officially remained an independent country, with its government intact, but to many residents it must have seemed like an occupied one. Japanese troops occupied the Royal Bangkok Sports Club (which, despite its predominantly

European membership, was nevertheless a Thai institution), as well as Lumpini Park and most other sites that offered open space for ammunition dumps. They took over the Oriental Hotel, which was managed by Tokyo's Imperial Hotel during the war years, and made free use of airports and railways. In January 1942 (after the fall of peninsular Malaya and most of the Philippines), the Thai government formally declared war on Britain and the US. The Thai ambassador in Washington, however, refused to deliver the declaration, which was ignored thereafter; in London, the story was different, with the result that the British, at least technically, regarded Thailand as an enemy.

In the last year or so of the war, when an invasion of Thailand was considered a distinct possibility (the Americans preferred to think of it as a liberation), a few bombs were dropped on Bangkok, mostly aimed at power stations and port facilities along the river. Wealthier families evacuated to the countryside, and some of the upmarket shops closed; an underground resistance group called the Free Thai began planning for an uprising which, had it occurred, would undoubtedly have been a bloody affair, since the Japanese were not only well armed but also quite aware of what was going on. In the event, of course, the atomic bomb was dropped, the Emperor made his famous broadcast, and the troops surrendered their guns with hardly a protest.

The city was in a sad state, with shortages of almost everything but rice. When a new group of owners acquired the Oriental Hotel, they found it stripped of bed linens, chinaware and even electric wiring, and had to assemble temporary furnishings piecemeal from shops in Chinatown. But all of the landmarks were intact; the trams still ran along New Road, and the city was still recognizable as itself.

Americans, for some reason, seemed to find it particularly beguiling. Perhaps this was because they were very much the heroes of the moment – they had come out on top in the matter of whether to treat Thailand as a liberated ally or as a defeated enemy – or perhaps there was something about the place that answered a certain need; at any rate, several of them decided to settle there and went on to make substantial contributions to the city's life.

Alexander Macdonald, for example, flew in with the OSS, the military intelligence group that later became the far more powerful CIA. 'Bangkok was an intriguing blend of old and new, East and West,' he recalled in a memoir that tried to explain its appeal:

> As a community, it tried on the things of modern civilization – electric power, fast automobiles, telephones, and public health campaigns – like a woman trying on hats, often times giggled at their absurdity and discarded them, relaxing to more informal ways of life. Bangkok was a wily, yet guileless city, always ready with new surprises. It was deeply devoted to the arts of pleasure. If nothing else, this would have been enough for me.

Jim Thompson, also with the OSS, was an architect by training who found the prospect of going back to a predictable, upper-class life on the East Coast of the US unappealing. The war had unleashed a new and unexpected taste for adventure, and ramshackle, chaotic Bangkok with its smiling people seemed to offer something different.

Both men found what they were looking for. With help from various sources (some of them American), Macdonald started up the *Bangkok Post*, which quickly became the main English-language newspaper. (Unfortunately, he fell foul of the government when Pibul returned to power after a brief period of post-war disgrace and was forced to leave in the 1950s.) Thompson, after an abortive try at renovating the Oriental Hotel, discovered the country's shimmering silks and made them internationally famous; he also built a Thai-style house, which is now one of Bangkok's leading tourist attractions. (He himself had a more dramatic end; while on an afternoon stroll

Jim Thompson's house.

in a Malaysian resort called the Cameron Highlands in 1967, he mysteriously vanished and has never been seen since.)

There was also an American who set up a bakery offering Thais the dubious pleasure of American-style bread, as well as American lawyers, American teachers, American businessmen and a whole bevy of American aid workers who got involved in everything from agriculture to rural health care. A surprising number of them found a home in Bangkok, quickly replacing the British as the predominant expatriate community.

One temporary resident who fell in love with the city was an American housewife called Carol Hollinger. Hollinger came in the mid-'50s, tried (and quickly failed) to adjust to the placid inbred world of embassy wives and then discovered an alternative lifestyle as a teacher at Chulalongkorn University. This she described in a book called *Mai Pen Rai Means Never Mind*, which, to me, is still the best account ever written of what it is actually like for a foreigner to live here. 'No road is straight in Bangkok,' she wrote, and the most ordinary pursuit has the habit of ending in extraordinary chaos. Americans complained and despaired and were made neurotic by this aspect of life in Bangkok. To me it was wild adventure to set out to a mundane party or on an innocent errand and to end up five hours later lost, hot, tired and desperate. I admit it doesn't sound like fun and it never was comfortable, but it was in these hot and hectic moments that I was most intensely aware that I had shed suburbia.

Hollinger's book was published in 1965, by which time she was tragically dead of a brain tumor. Strangely, most Thais at the university, where I was then teaching, were offended by it. They thought that she was making jokes at their expense and were quite unable to see that what she had produced was a passionate, book-length love letter.

Indirectly, Americans were largely responsible for the startling transformation of Bangkok over the next few decades. The money they poured in, first in the form of conventional aid and soon, starting in the mid-'60s, in support of the war in Vietnam, produced a new class of instant millionaires, not all of them military, and initiated a building boom that only ended, perhaps temporarily, with the economic crash of 1997.

The role of the Vietnam War in Thailand's prosperity is a sensitive point with many Thais. Some of them deny any connection at all. One, a high-ranking diplomat then serving with the United Nations, asked me for lunch to refute a fairly innocuous article I had written for an American newspaper in the late '60s about all of the changes in Bangkok, which, I inferred, were a by-product of the war effort. This was false, he said firmly; the country was booming because of sound economic policies; in no material way, none at all, was it profiting from the conflict just across its borders.

Well, perhaps. But there were certainly a lot of crew-cut young Americans suddenly on the streets with money to spend, and an unusual number of entertainment places appeared with remarkable speed to cater to their needs.

It *would* be wrong to suggest, as many have done, that Bangkok's celebrated sex industry was a product of the Vietnam War. As in every other large Asian city (and in small ones as well), sex had always been there, and the industry was not solely (or even primarily) aimed at foreign visitors. In the pre-war days, most of it was based in Chinatown, where there were numerous licensed brothels, as well as (until 1959) legal opium dens and 'tea houses' with rooms for rent above; others could be found elsewhere, like the floating brothels of Klong Saen Saeb and the establishments along Soi Klang off Sukhumwit Road. Massage parlours were not unknown, as the card handed to Somerset Maugham and his friend indicates. At a somewhat higher level, there were 'hostess clubs' where the girls had to be taken out, preferably after a decent interval, to any number of discreet 'short-time' hotels. Along Ratchadamnoen Avenue, when I arrived in 1960, there were several large 'day clubs' patronized by government officials before they went home in the evening.

As early as 1956, *A Woman of Bangkok* by Jack Reynolds pioneered literary themes that would become more or less standard for writers attempting to explore the city's charms. Like nearly all of the later examples of this genre, it tells the story of an innocent young *farang* (in this case, an Englishman) who sinks into the city's iniquitous pleasures and finally emerges, sadder but wiser in a whole spectrum of new erotic ways. A few years later, *Emmanuelle* appeared, supposedly written by its eponymous heroine, but actually the work of a Frenchman employed by the United Nations. The original book caused little stir (it was actually banned in France in a brief flush of Gaullist prudery), but the movie version was an international sensation and confirmed impressions of Bangkok as a seething centre of sexual adventure.

Sex in general was something the Thais took for granted without a great deal of bother and discussion. Girls of good family were strictly chaperoned before marriage – I could not have a well-born unmarried woman of 38 to my house for dinner without also asking a respectable married couple known to her parents – but almost everybody else was free to do as he or she liked. Though polygamy had been abolished, every man who could afford it had a few 'minor wives' whom he set up in households of their own; when a military strongman died in the early '60s, nobody was surprised when it came out (in a dispute over property) that he had more than 80 of these, though there was some criticism when it was discovered that he had appropriated millions from the national treasury to pay for them.

However, sex undeniably became more public in the 1960s and early '70s, when entirely new centres sprang up. These were anything but discreet: bars with names like Pussy Galore and Nudie, palatial massage parlours at which a customer selected the girl of his choice through one-way windows and took her upstairs for all sorts of 'special services', scores of little, dark, hole-in-the-wall places where live-action shows of astonishing dexterity were offered. Gay bars were almost as numerous as straight ones; even in the latter, it took a practised eye to tell the difference between actual girls and equally pretty transvestites.

Many of these places were on or near Patpong Road, a privately-owned thoroughfare between Silom and Suriwong Roads that had previously been devoted to travel agencies, restaurants and a few sedate piano bars. Almost overnight, it seemed, Patpong and its vicinity became a garish blaze of neon lights and amplified noise, packed nightly with foreign men and Thai girls. Another popular centre was on New Petchburi Road, while another, dubbed Soi Cowboy, grew up at the corner of Sukhumwit and Soi Asoke. In the beginning, these new places were aimed almost exclusively at the young Americans who came to Bangkok on rest-and-recreation leave from the horrors of the battlefield. Itineraries, organized by local entrepreneurs, were anything but subtle. One five-day deal that I saw, offered, for a remarkably low sum, an air-conditioned hotel room, a girl of one's choice (exchangeable if unsatisfactory), a tailor-made suit, several meals and a morning tour of the Grand Palace and the Temple of the Emerald Buddha (the tour, I was told, was seldom taken). But most of them outlived the war. The day of mass tourism happily dawned about the time when the military customers were leaving, and their places on the bar stools and massage parlour couches were taken by middle-aged men from all parts of the world, entranced to discover that a pot-belly and thinning hair meant nothing to the crowds of dazzling young beauties clamouring for their attention.

There was a dark side to all this, of course, even before the shadow of AIDS loomed. Thousands of girls (and boys, too), some of them very young indeed, flooded into Bangkok from the provinces to make what must have seemed easy money compared with labouring in the family rice fields. There were depressing stories of families who sold their daughters into prostitution. Crime flourished, much of it committed by policemen who controlled the entertainment districts. And drugs came on the scene, not used much by Thais themselves in the beginning, but readily available to others as they passed through *en route* from the Golden Triangle in the far north to eager markets abroad.

Together with these developments, Bangkok was swept by a building boom. It began rather tentatively with the first Western-style supermarkets, the first air-conditioned shopping centres, the first (mostly Japanese) department stores. Then, in the late 1970s, it really took off.

For many years, it had been assumed that the city's soft, wet soil – in most areas, the water level was less than a metre below the surface – would not accommodate the sort of tall buildings going up in Hong Kong and Singapore; hence the largely flat skyline, with only a few structures rising above four or five storeys. When the Oriental Hotel built a new wing in the late 1950s, it had the city's first lift, regarded as a marvel and not a very reliable one either; Eleanor Roosevelt, on an official visit, got stuck in it for an hour or so soon after it was installed.

But new construction techniques solved this problem, and local builders made up for lost time. The Dusit Thani Hotel was one of the first highrises, towering over Lumpini Park; others quickly followed. Few were in the older sections, where land was scarce or owned by the government, but they shot up almost everywhere else. Though from time to time, there has been solemn talk about 'residential zones' and 'green belts', nothing of the sort has ever really been taken seriously in Bangkok, or not so seriously that it could not be quietly scrapped by the next government. At one point, for example, Wireless Road, a handsome street lined with rain trees and home to several embassies, was proclaimed to be 'residential'. For this reason, a row of what looked suspiciously like commercial buildings announced that they were, in fact, 'town houses', and an existing hotel nearby was refused permission to build a high-rise extension. This lasted but a short time. The buildings did indeed become shops, and the hotel was torn down and replaced with a much larger new one; now, Wireless is lined with some of the most desirable office buildings in the city, casting perpetual shadows over the leafy gardens of the American and Dutch ambassadorial residences.

To visitors returning to Bangkok after an absence of only a few years, the change was startling, and for newcomers expecting a languid *King and I* atmosphere, it was both a shock and a revelation. The travel writer Robert D. Kaplan, who arrived in the early '90s straight from India, saw the city as his 'first encounter with the Asian economic miracle'. It seemed that 'building and road construction was a twenty-four-hour-a-day activity,' with the constant sound of power drills and jackhammers. Few of the new office blocks, banks, hotels, condominiums and shopping centres that resulted from all of this activity have any architectural distinction (some of them are frankly jokes, like the so-called Robot Building and a condo on the river that manages to incorporate no fewer than six different European styles), but they are certainly numerous and certainly large.

The tallest is Baiyoke Tower 2, occupying a relatively small piece of land in Pratunam near Baiyoke Tower 1 (formerly the tallest), but other examples loom along Silom Road and on the west bank of the Chao Phraya. One of the weirdest collections rises abruptly like gravestones out of former rice fields north of the airport; known as Muang Thong Thani ('Heavenly Golden City'), this was envisaged by a developer as a self-contained little city, with its own residential towers and shops, all in the middle of nowhere. Nobody apparently lives there, or at least not very many people do, and wastepaper blows through the empty streets.

A question I have sometimes idly asked, without receiving a very satisfactory answer, is why on earth so many enormous condominiums and apartment houses were built in such a brief time. In 1982, according to a survey, there were 48 condo projects in the entire country; by 1992, there were 220 going up in Bangkok alone, most of them 30 storeys or taller. I do not know a single well-to-do Thai family (the only kind who could afford such places) who lives in one of them out of choice or who aspires to do so. A few foreigners have bought units (despite an intimidating list of complicated legal requirements), and many expatriates live in rented apartments, mainly because most of the houses they would prefer have been torn down. A large number of such buildings, though, especially in Thon Buri, remain half-empty and seem likely to stay that way. I am forced to the conclusion – in which I would probably be supported by a number of unhappy bankers – that they were built simply because the land was there and because someone was eager to lend the builders some money.

One inevitable result of all of this building activity, and of all of the money that seemed to be pouring into Bangkok, was that the traffic got much worse. This is not to say that there was no traffic before; within a decade of New Road's construction, as we have seen, people were complaining about the congestion,

Bus riders in traffic.

and they have been doing so ever since. During the Vietnam War, it was commonly said that if the Vietnamese ever invaded, they would be stopped dead in the city's suburbs by motionless masses of automobiles, trucks, buses, mini-vans, motorcycles and little three-wheeled vehicles known as *tuk-tuks*; at least one thoughtful hostess always put D.O.T. (Depending on Traffic) below the time on her invitation cards.

But in the boom-time '80s and '90s, the number of motor vehicles undeniably increased, to such an extent that by 1998, 90 per cent of all of those registered in Thailand were in the capital. No article on Bangkok fails to mention the traffic, and some Thais even derive a perverse pleasure in telling you how impossible it is. ('Worse than New York! Worse than Los Angeles! Worse than anywhere!') It can take hours to go a short distance, especially when the dread FPR (Friday, Payday, Rain) factor is added to the normal problems, even more when the rain is of the kind that puts major arteries under a half metre or more of water. One beat-the-traffic enterprise that has developed is the motorcycle taxi. These are operated by groups of young drivers who gather at strategic points all over the city and offer hair-raising rides to fares, weaving through cars and occasionally taking shortcuts on public sidewalks. They are obviously popular; I regularly see mature women, men in business suits with briefcases, and bar girls in evening gowns perched precariously on the backs of such machines.

Every government for at least 40 years has pledged to do something about the traffic; one minister a few years ago rashly said he would solve the problem in only six months and then, when the period passed with no discernable improvement, confessed that it was beyond the powers of any human endeavour. At the end of 1999, however, something *was* actually done, and while the problem is still severe, there is now an alternative on certain notoriously congested routes.

On the King's birthday that year (always a popular time for starting up such things), the Bangkok Sky Train opened. For ages, most of Sukhumwit Road and parts of Silom and Sathorn had been construction sites, adding to the congestion and occasionally causing damage when chunks of cement and steel fell on cars below. Most people thought this would go on forever, like the plans for a new airport which have been through at least six governments, or be abandoned halfway through, like a project for a monorail to Don Muang started by a company called Hopewell ('Hopeless' as it was soon known). But in what seemed like a miracle, the Sky Train did get finished, it did open, and it is running.

The number of customers has been disappointing because it is too expensive for the great majority of Bangkok's commuters (20 to 40 *baht* as opposed to only 2 or 3 for a bus travelling the same distance), but for those who use it there are surprising new views of the city. Behind those identical walls of dingy row-shops, it turns out, there are wonderful old mansions

The Sky Train at Nana Station.

hidden in overgrown gardens; at night, the floodlit green fields of the exclusive Sports Club are transformed into a very public spectacle of rugby and tennis players going about their games; even familiar landmarks like the Victory Monument look different when seen from an elevation. You can also go all the way from the outer reaches of Sukhumwit to the wonderful Weekend Market without encountering a single traffic jam, in just ten or fifteen minutes.

An even more daring innovation, an underground system, is being built and is scheduled to open in 2004; passing the miles of machinery along Rama IV Road, one of its routes, taxi drivers shake their heads in wonder and cheerfully speculate about how many passengers will go to a watery death in the first really bad flood.

Also prominently visible from the Sky Train are many of the three-hundred-odd unfinished high-rise buildings that blight the Bangkok skyline, some shrouded in plastic sheets, others rusty skeletons that seem about to collapse. These are victims of the 1997 Asian financial meltdown, an epidemic that first appeared in Thailand before spreading to other countries, transforming many new billionaires into new paupers almost overnight. The non-stop construction spree came to a grinding halt as builders were unable to pay workers or find additional funds. Finance companies closed abruptly, factories folded, banks revealed a staggering load of non-performing loans and for a few months foreign journalists got entertaining copy out of a 'Market of the Recently Rich' which sprang up on Sukhumwit Soi 55, offering Rolex watches, Mercedes Benz sports cars, speed boats and the odd private plane, all at bargain prices.

But the market soon closed (with most of its items unsold), and, despite many headlines about financial skullduggery, nobody went to jail (or at least no-one has yet). The uncompleted buildings were just abandoned, perhaps to be continued, perhaps not; nobody seems to know or to want to make much of an issue about it. New, expensive automobiles appeared on the streets after a brief absence; the glossy shopping centres

An unfinished high-rise block.

with their Gucci, Vuitton, Prada and Chanel outlets were soon
as busy as ever; new restaurants continued to open and, apparently, to flourish. If you did not notice all of those silent
construction sites slowly rotting away in the tropical sunlight,
you would never know that Bangkok had any more problems
than it had had in the past.

There is presently some discussion about an ambitious
preservation plan for old Bangkok, meaning the original island
fortress containing the Grand Palace, Wat Po, Sanam Luang, the
City Shrine and other landmarks. Under this proposal, which is
estimated to take sixteen years to realize, all modern structures
in the area will be removed, vistas will be restored, and, its
adherents claim, tourists will be able to experience the purely
Thai atmosphere of Rama I.

There is, needless to say, a contrary view. Critics say that the project will result in a fraudulent Disneyland creation, devoid of the life and spirit that makes the area truly Thai. However, they ignore the facts that nearly all of the structures to be removed are singularly hideous, that, after dark, Sanam Luang has become the haunt of drug addicts, homeless people and prostitutes, and that much of the 'life' there is provided by tourists and students of Thammasat and Silpakorn Universities. The debate will probably go on forever. Bangkok, after all, has a long history of shrugging off efforts at sensible planning, one that is, paradoxically, a major part of its appeal.

11 The City Today

Though I have lived in Bangkok for more than 40 years and consider it my home, I remain, like every other foreign resident I know, unavoidably an outsider. This is not, I think, due to any particular attitude of the Thais; perhaps because they have never been suspicious of Westerners, perhaps just because they are naturally among the most hospitable people in the world, I have only rarely felt the cultural and social isolation that friends who live in, say, Japan and China sometimes complain about. Still, there are large areas of Thai experience that I know I will never be able to enter in any but a superficial way and thus will never truly understand.

I feel that this is a necessary prelude to the observations that follow. Some of them may be downright wrong (though never intentionally so), and nearly all are incomplete. I am constantly discovering new aspects of the city, sometimes completely new areas, and revising long-held generalizations about its people in the face of conflicting evidence. The process is continuous and never-ending, as is possibly true of any great city, but more so in a culture not one's own.

Take these impressions, then, for what they are and nothing more, merely one foreigner's view of the infinitely complex and always changing city around him.

One initial impression that has not changed over the years is of the vastness of the place. The Bangkok Metropolitan Area now covers 1,537 sq km on both sides of the Chao Phraya River, a figure I got from an official publication, but which, like most Thai statistics, may or may not be true; another hundred or so kilometres have probably been added since that survey was made. The Metropolitan Area sprawls all the way to the gulf, nearly all the way to Ayutthaya; even when you technically leave it, there are few visual signs to suggest any significant change in the surroundings. One of the things that makes it seem even larger is that so many of the newer areas lack any identifiable landmarks, any particular cluster of buildings that proclaims itself as a centre; naked streets stretch as far as the eye can see across an absolutely flat plain.

You learn a few areas, of course, in the course of daily life, and the old ones have remained more or less the same for the past 50 years. There are points of reference in some of these, such as the Grand Palace, famous temples, the more established hotels, Lumpini Park. But the greater part of Bangkok has grown up within the past twenty years, during which time the population has doubled or tripled and suburbs have crept out in all directions over what many residents recall as rice fields and orchards.

Get off the overhead expressway at one of the more distant ramps, still within the city, and you are likely to have no idea where you are. It all looks much the same: perhaps a few tall buildings from the boom years, nowadays more often than not only half finished, but otherwise the familiar row-shops that look as though they were assembled from a do-it-yourself architecture kit (which in a sense they were), even the newer ones streaked with stains and dust from wide new roads that seem perpetually under construction. Every now and then, you see a suggestion that the owner has aspired to bit of originality — by painting the whole construction bright pink or lemon yellow, by adding a few incongruous wrought-iron balconies, in one case by installing a model of the Eiffel Tower on the roof — but nothing can really change the row-shops' basic similarity or intrinsic ugliness. They are not made to last, still less to enhance, but to perform a simple, commercial function.

There is life in these nowhere places, though. People do have businesses in them, go to schools, play sports in vacant lots, have homes somewhere behind the row-shop façades. Even if

104

they appear on few city maps (which are, incidentally, hopeless when it comes to the outer suburbs), there are long, straight roads of semi-detached houses, each one representing the fulfillment of a dream to own a bit of land, even if it means paying for it in a long series of monthly payments. Other roads suggest affluence in that the houses are larger, separate and often display two or three automobiles parked within stout gates. But even here, there is no sense of a community, of being in a distinct neighbourhood; you feel that the roads could vanish as suddenly as they appeared, leaving no trace.

One reason, I think, that much of Bangkok has so little visual charm and such a generally functional atmosphere is that it is really a southern Chinese creation, reflecting the tastes of comparatively recent immigrants unaccustomed to the idea of permanence and with no particular aesthetic sensibility. This may be a controversial statement, one apt to be misunderstood, so I should stress that I am speaking of attitudes and social values, not of citizenship or loyalty. Nearly every Chinese in

In Chinatown.

Bangkok today is Thai by nationality with a Thai name and an obvious stake in the country's future; at the Immigration Department, where foreigners must go for the annual renewal of their residence permits, you rarely see any of the once numerous old-fashioned, identifiably Chinese people, frail old men and women in black silk trousers patiently signing the numerous forms with a fingerprint mark under the supervision of smartly dressed grandchildren. Campaigns with slogans like 'Proud to be Thai' and 'Buy Thai' are, for the most part, launched by department stores whose Chinese owners are genuinely proud of their contribution.

It was not always so, however. The first wave of immigrants in the nineteenth century, and often their descendents, too, proudly proclaimed their racial identity. In a book entitled *Twentieth Century Impressions of Siam*, one of a series issued in 1908 by a British publisher, nearly all of the non-European business leaders have Chinese names (Lee Cheng Chan, for instance, and Li Tit Guan) and are pictured in Chinese dress outside palatial Chinese-style mansions near their rice mills and trading companies. Even later, when a Thai name became requisite for those who wanted citizenship, one was generally adopted only for official purposes, with the old names still used in society and commerce.

The Chinese lived, too, at a certain distance from their Thai hosts, and not just physically in Chinatown and on the west bank of the river. From the provinces of south China where most of them originated, they brought their secretive triads, their ancestral shrines, their schools, their clan houses that found jobs for new arrivals and took care of needy old people. In the pre-war days, many also retained their Chinese citizenship or acquired British and American papers, which enabled them to avoid Thai military conscription and to be tried in foreign courts.

It is not true, as some present-day Sino-Thais like to believe, that there has never been overtly anti-Chinese sentiment in Thailand. King Rama VI, as we have seen, expressed a decidedly dim view of Chinese economic power, although his attitude towards the local community seems to have been mixed. On the one hand, he was the first Thai King to award honourary noble titles to individual Chinese, especially to those who made donations to his various projects. On the other hand, as part of his policy to promote nationalism, many of his writings attacked them for not being 'true Thai'. According to Walter Vella, one of his biographers,

> The Thai tendency not to regard the Chinese as foreigners arose, said the King, out of Thai lack of understanding of Siam's long-range interests. The Chinese were a convenience: they worked hard for little pay. The Thai were too ready to accept the easy way. As a result the Thai had become dependent on the Chinese. This dependence had made many Thai reluctant to look at the problem that had arisen, to balk at saying anything critical about the Chinese. Such dependence, which led some Thai to say 'If the Chinese go on strike again, we will all die,' was woeful. Other Thai asserted that if the Chinese were not counted as Thai, there would be few Thai left to count at all. Not true [said the King]. The congestion of Chinese in Bangkok gave a false picture, for in the countryside the Chinese were not numerous and, further, were much less Chinese.

In the late 1930s, the military government of Field Marshal Pibul took a number of more overtly discriminatory measures. The change of the country's name, for example, was an effort to stress the ethnic primacy of the Thais over minorities. In 1942 certain occupations like law, charcoal production and the making of Buddha images were reserved for Thais; even when I first arrived, only Thais were allowed to be barbers and taxi drivers, though enforcement by that time was not very stringent. Pibul also virtually stopped Chinese immigration and imposed strict controls on Chinese associations, schools and newspapers. The majority of the Bangkok Chinese at that time

New Year in Chinatown, 2001.

probably had somewhat ambivalent feelings about the city as a home. Many had long been sending large sums of money out to support families on the mainland, allied themselves politically with either the Koumintang or the Communists and were openly anti-Japanese when the official policy was conciliatory. (One of the first buildings occupied by the Japanese when they entered Bangkok in 1941 was the Chinese Chamber of Commerce, which they used as their main military headquarters. One of the first revenge killings, just days after the surrender in 1945, was of the head of the Chamber, who had allegedly collaborated with the Japanese.)

All of this began to change after the war. In part, it was simply a question of good business and of adjusting to realities. Finding themselves at odds with the powerful military establishment, which was (and remains) almost wholly Thai, Chinese bankers and businessmen resolved the problem by appointing high officers as directors, thus in effect making them allies as well as very rich. In part, too, it was caused by mainland politics; few of the wealthier Chinese supported the Communist government when it took over back home, and the outward flow of money became a relative trickle. (Though it has by no means stopped; several of the larger Sino-Thai companies have found that they can work with the new China and now probably earn more from it than they do from the new Thailand.)

Finally, and most importantly, the situation was caused by increasing intermarriage, which blurred the racial picture to such a degree that, at least in Bangkok, it would be impossible to sort out the different strands. This process had actually started long before with the arrival of the first immigrants, nearly all of them single men, in the nineteenth century and their marrying of local women, but it accelerated at a rapid pace as the idea of an ancestral homeland began to recede.

At the highest levels, an impoverished Thai aristocrat might marry a wealthy Chinese woman who wanted to improve her social status, bringing mutual benefits to each. Such marriages are nearly always successful, and there is little comment on the element of calculation that brings them about. Older Chinese families also branched out, embracing Thai sons – and daughters-in-law, and their children, in turn, continued the process. Thus there is no longer any easy way to identify the minority as there is, for example, in countries like Indonesia and Malaysia, where religious differences discourage such alliances. In the mid-1960s, it is estimated that up to 300,000 people, mostly Chinese, were slaughtered in Java and Bali, and Malaysia today has numerous laws giving preference to Malays in schools and government jobs. Nothing like this would be imaginable in Bangkok, if only because such a large part of the population has at least some Chinese blood, often quite a bit.

The local response to even raising the subject, quite fairly, would be to say that it makes no difference, that just as America's numerous minorities have become American, so the Chinese in Thailand have become Thai; it is a question not of race but of nationality. If Chinese New Year (not celebrated as an official holiday) still finds most of the smaller shops closed and the streets largely empty of traffic, the big supermarkets and department stores remain open, and it is no longer a time to stock up on basic supplies, as it was 20 or 30 years ago. If old Chinatown still remains a world closed to non-Chinese, it is also true that most of its more prosperous residents long ago opened businesses and built houses in other areas. If you still hear the noisy crackle of fireworks and receive a moon cake on traditional Chinese occasions, it now seems merely a part of general life.

And it is indeed a part: as far as Bangkok is concerned, the result of this successful assimilation has been the steady decline, virtually the disappearance, of anything purely Thai. Except for the Buddhist temples and the Grand Palace, hardly a single classical Thai structure remains; nor, if we compare the city with a typical village in, say, the central or northern regions, is there much that could be called authentic Thai culture. Official committees (often themselves largely composed of Sino-Thais) can coin new expressions like 'ekkalot thai' ('Thai Identity'), issue publications stressing 'Thai' characteristics and generally strive to promote such concepts, but they have little relevance to what you see and experience all around you in Bangkok.

The high walls that surround private houses (often studded with broken glass as an added deterrent to intruders), the taste for ostentatious display (enormous gilded gates, rooms filled with ornate furniture in a style vaguely called 'Louis' that nobody ever seems to sit on), the indifference to community affairs (any proposed group effort to clean up a neglected public street or polluted canal is regarded as eccentric if not downright lunatic), the tendency to shout even in casual conversations and (on a more positive note) the drive and energy behind most successful businesses — all of these are Chinese, not Thai. And the outsider who seeks to generalize about Thai values and attitudes without ever leaving the city (as countless writers have done) is likely to produce as distorted a picture as one who attempted a similar assessment of America on the basis of a stay in New York City.

Of course, there are real Thais in Bangkok, millions of them perhaps, but with few exceptions they have little effect on the city's physical appearance or on its real power structure. Look in the glossy pages of the *Thailand Tatler*, to take but one example; almost every socially prominent face is plainly Chinese; the same is true in the executive offices of big banks and business firms, the private clubs, the classrooms of the better schools and universities. In a recent letter to the *Bangkok Post*, a reader called attention to the fact that nearly all of the incumbent government's cabinet members were Chinese, an observation that drew not a single rebuttal.

No sinister conclusions should be drawn from this. It is merely a fact of modern Thai life. But it is one that needs to be kept in mind in any discussions about both city and country.

A large number of Bangkok residents who are not Chinese are villagers, people who have come from somewhere else. Many, perhaps most, will never go back, but their hearts remain in the villages; they constantly call to them in their dreams and provide a standard against which to judge the bewildering ways of this strange place. Ask a taxi driver 'Where is your home?' and nine times out of ten he will reply 'Roi Et' or 'Yasothorn' or some other distant province; ask him if he misses it, and he will assure you he does, all the time.

Let us take one of these migrants and call him Tongkham. His village is in the far north, in a small province somewhere near the borders of Burma and Laos, and for most of his early life he spoke only the northern dialect, quite different from the one used in central Thailand. He has seven brothers and sisters, an average-sized family in the countryside, where many hands are needed to persuade rice to grow in sometimes not very fertile soil and where there is an old tradition of several children dying young.

111

The village of Tongkham's childhood, 50 years ago, had no electricity, no regular water supply, no paved roads; the only medical clinic was in the provincial capital, 30 km away, and the level of competence there was such that most people preferred the herbal remedies of their ancestors. Spiritual guidance and social life were centred on the local *wat*, where festivals and other events were held, and whose abbot was often called on to arbitrate in local disputes. Tongkham attended a district school for five years, learning to read and write but not much else, before he left to help in the family fields full time.

But he does not recall those days as hardship. On the contrary, he looks back on them as a golden time and returns to the village at every opportunity — at Songkran, the old Thai New Year, for example, for the cremation of a relation or close family friend, or just because he misses the warmth of life there and wants to recapture it for a weekend. When his parents died, he inherited the family house and land, but unlike many of Bangkok's other ex-villagers he has held on to them despite temptations to sell; one of his sisters lives there now with her family, and they still grow rice, though they enjoy such modern amenities as electricity and — a recent addition — a telephone.

Tongkham decided to try his luck in Bangkok when he was barely eighteen years old. This might seem an unusual decision for a young man who had spent all of his life in a distant village and never even visited nearby provincial capitals like Chiang Mai and Chiang Rai, but in fact it was happening all over Thailand. New highways were being built everywhere in the '60s, bus services had become regular and cheap, and new job opportunities were opening up in and around the capital. Moreover, with improved medical services, the infant mortality rate was dropping; there was a surplus of young mouths feed, an added reason for families to break apart.

Poorer regions like the arid north-east were particularly vulnerable to the big city's traditional allure, and certain provinces (Roi Et and Yasothorn, for example) lost virtually all

Warehouse scenes.

of their able-bodied people between the ages of fifteen and thirty. Luckier ones found work in factories where they were provided with a place to live, sometimes with a decent wage and a degree of security. Others laboured on construction sites (moving from one to another as projects were completed), drove taxis and *tuk-tuks*, became servants in wealthy homes or waiters in restaurants, and provided the largest number of recruits for the booming sex industry.

Tongkham worked first as a gardener, the lowest-paid member of the household staff of a colonel in the army. Then, through a friend who had come from the same village, he got an almost equally low-ranking job with a Chinese-owned company that produced water filters. But he was hard-working, perhaps a little brighter and more ambitious than the average, and gradually made his way up to a position as a repairman, going all over Bangkok by motorcycle and getting to know the city well.

He got married, to a girl from the north-east who sold *som-tam*, a spicy green-papaya salad, in a market, but this was unsuccessful. She was lazy, he says, and possibly not faithful; even worse, they could not seem to have children. After a few years, they drifted apart and eventually agreed to get a divorce, which, in Thailand, is simply a matter of going down to a government office and signing an official document.

By this time, Tongkham had risen to salesman, learned a bit of English at one of Bangkok's numerous language schools and had a small staff (including two of his younger brothers) to assist in making his rounds of potential water-filter customers. He had become an expert in his narrow field, knowing a good deal about assorted chemicals used in the filters and also about related products like water heaters. His salary amounted to only around 3,000 *baht* a month (about $150 at the time), but it was enough to pay for a rented room in a semi-slum, send a few hundred *baht* a month home to his elderly parents and go out for an occasional evening on the town with friends.

Like most of the city's transplanted villagers, Tongkham maintained close contact with others who came from the same province and depended on them for most of his social life. They got together frequently to eat familiar foods, pass on stories from home and speak their regional dialect. You might think that a lifetime of exposure to central Thai on national television and radio would have gradually reduced the popularity of such dialects, but this has not been the case; sharing the same jokes with friends in what amounts to almost a different language is a way of relieving the stress of living in a place that will always seem fundamentally strange.

In the early '90s, like many Thais, not only in Bangkok but in other larger cities, Tongkham was seized with a desire to have his own business, with a proper office, proper calling cards and a chance of real success. The times seemed propitious for such a venture: banks were generous about lending money; new private hospitals and companies needed industrial-size water filters; there was every reason to believe that the good times would go on forever. So Tongkham borrowed some funds, rented an office, persuaded his two brothers (both by now married with children) to join him and became a legally regis-tered company.

All of this was much less impressive than it sounds. The office consisted of two crowded rooms on the ground floor of a shop-house, many other companies were offering the same product (regularly cutting prices to make a sale), and the brothers had to work hard seven days a week just to make ends meet. At times, big sales seem tantalizingly near, but somehow they always failed to materialize due to rising costs, unexpected taxes like VAT and increasingly tough competition.

The business struggled on until 1998, when it became one of the countless casualties of Thailand's economic crisis, hardly worth recording amid the crash of so many major companies. Tongkham's brothers found other ways to support their fami-lies; one went back to the village and farming, while the other set up a roadside stall in Bangkok selling food.

A backstreet scene.

Tongkham debated whether he should go back himself. Doing so, however, would have been an admission of defeat in the big city (a loss of face, too, because having his own company had given him a certain status in the village) and, moreover, at a time when, by Thai standards, he was well past middle age. Instead, like thousands of others, he became a taxi driver, differing from the majority only in that he owns his own vehicle (paying for it in monthly instalments) and thus can maintain some illusion of independence.

He likes meeting new people, enjoys driving and knows the back streets of Bangkok better than most of its natives. Since his parents are now dead and he no longer has to send money home, he can earn a basic living. But, in his estimation (and society's, too) being any kind of driver is a low-ranking occupation, not one to be proud of, certainly not what he hoped for in the years of youthful struggle. Maybe he will do it for a little longer and then go back to the village of his dreams; maybe he will become a monk and spend the rest of his life in quiet meditation; maybe he will just stay on in the city, though he will never consider it his real home.

More than half of Bangkok's population is under the age of 30; this official statistic is readily believable when you look at the youthful faces around you on any street. They come from all parts of the country to seek work, to enjoy the city's plentiful amusements or, in many cases, to get an education.

While a number of universities have opened in provincial regions, all the older, more prestigious ones (Chulalongkorn, Thammasat, Kasetsart, and Mahidol) are in Bangkok; so are Silpakorn (fine arts), Srinakharinwirot (education), Assumption (business and accounting), and huge Ramkhamhaeng, an 'open' university that requires no entrance examination and has tens of thousands of students. In addition, there are countless vocational schools as well as private ones that specialize in preparing students for university entrance, or teach useful subjects like foreign languages and computer skills. It would be untrue to say that Bangkok is the only place in Thailand to get a decent education, but the great majority of Thais believe that the best opportunities are here, and provincial families are often willing to make considerable sacrifices so that their children have a chance to try their luck in the city.

University students today are different from the ones I used to lecture to 40 years ago. Then, they belonged to a relatively small, élite group, wearing modest uniforms that disguised social differences, observing such traditional Thai behaviour patterns as sitting meekly in class, offering a polite, prayer-like salute whenever I passed and rarely asking questions or offering an opinion of their own. ('If they ask you a question,' an older Thai colleague told me, 'it means that you haven't been clear and that would be an implied criticism. Which of course is contrary to everything they've been taught.')

Now when I go to Siam Square and its nearby shopping centres, popular places to hang out, I hardly recognize students in their fancy, attention-demanding attire: ungainly platform shoes and imitation (or maybe genuine) Prada bags for the girls, baggy pants and sometimes orange hair for the boys, mobile phones for all, constantly beeping, buzzing or playing snatches of 'Home Sweet Home' or 'Auld Lang Syne'. Even the girls who are compelled to wear uniforms often adapt them with a fashionable touch.

But between those silent, diligent students of the past and the sophisticated, seemingly frivolous ones of today, there was another generation that was neither mute nor devoted to pleasure and that led a kind of revolution.

Suddenly (or so it seemed to some of us at the time), they developed a social conscience, inspired no doubt by their counterparts in Europe and America, perhaps by the popular songs they had taken to singing in groups on campus. They protested against the flood of Japanese goods that was inundating the Thai market (seeing nothing ironic in the fact that they were compelled to use Japanese amplifiers in their campaign) and against the slaughter of wild animals in national parks by military hunters and ultimately, in a logical progression, against the seemingly omnipotent military government itself. In October 1973, through massive demonstrations at Thammasat University and around the Democracy Monument (carrying large pictures of the royal family to show their allegiance to at least one important aspect of the status quo), they succeeded in bringing down the government and sending three of its top leaders into temporary exile. It was a heady moment in Thai affairs, a rare, genuinely popular uprising, the first of several that would shake the region.

Stern young faces dominated the front pages of the newspapers, demanding radical change; the National Lottery, an alleged centre of corruption, was burned down; when the Bangkok police retreated in panic to their barracks, Boy Scouts solemnly (and quite efficiently) took over traffic control for a few days; the rector of Thammasat was appointed interim Prime Minister. Even the city's vocational students, normally regarded as a rowdy group who fought mostly among themselves, emerged as heroes, having appointed themselves protectors to their more cerebral university comrades.

In the end, these events proved only a temporary deviation from the old Thai preference for strong leadership and deep distrust of social confrontation. Three years of sometimes violent labour disputes, constant hectoring by student leaders, and (most frightening of all) Communist takeovers in Cambodia, Vietnam and Laos produced an inevitable backlash led by right-wing military officers and most of the Sino-Thai business élite. (The vocational students also switched sides, joining a group of super patriots called the Red Guards and thus ending an alliance that was never natural or close.) This was the era of the 'domino theory', and the withdrawal of American military forces from Thailand in 1975 left many in the country feeling very insecure. (Several *farang* friends of mine, convinced that the end was at hand, moved away; there were rumours that some rich Thais were quietly shifting their assets to safer havens; rumours indeed were the common currency of the day, the most incredible of them passed on in breathless telephone calls always prefaced by the remark 'I've got this from a very reliable source.')

In 1976, again in October, a frenzied mob descended on Thammasat, where yet another demonstration was in progress, and within a few hours slaughtered a still-undetermined number of students. Television films, aired late that afternoon but never again, showed young men being beaten and hung from the tamarind trees around Sanam Luang, others (girls as well as boys) stripped and forced to crawl on their bellies inside the university grounds.

The event, though predicted by many, shocked even those who had deliberately whipped it up with inflammatory rumours about Communists and supposedly anti-royal senti-ments. Whatever their political views might have been, the students, after all, came predominantly from middle- and upper-class families and were regarded as Thailand's future leaders. And such public violence was a very rare occurrence, then or now, very un-Thai. Even during *coups d'états*, things were usually resolved with a brief show of force, a flurry of headlines, and then it was business as usual. This time, a kind of stunned sense of revulsion fell over the city, and it lasted a long time. A new, reactionary government was appointed; of course, after a year, it was duly overthrown and the military returned to power, though in a much more subdued form. Some of the student leaders fled into the jungles of the northeast, along the Laos border, where they joined small groups of real Communists and possibly took part in activities against the Thai army. A few years later, though, an amnesty was declared, and most of them calmly resumed their studies as if nothing had happened. Many went on to become teachers and politicians, among them several members of future governments. Every October, a memorial service is held at Thammasat, and a small group of survivors and relatives of those whose bodies were never found agitates for an investigation of what really happened that day, of who was really responsible. But few expect anything to come of this; the Thais are generally not eager to examine controversial episodes in their past or to open doors behind which ugly secrets may lie.

Now the students (like those elsewhere) seem apathetic, less idealistic, more concerned with having a good time and getting a good job after graduation. They gather at places like Siam Square or in countless pubs and discos; they sometimes take recreational drugs like Ecstasy and amphetamines; they attend rock concerts and chat on the Internet. A few can still be stirred to political action, as they showed in the early '90s when they joined successful demonstrations against an attempted military takeover of the, by then, democratic government; but this time, they were only a part of a crowd of mostly middle-class businessmen and played no significant role.

A surprising number of the young people in Bangkok are homosexual, at least if you can believe reports in the local press. Certainly, there is a lot more chatter about the subject than there used to be, and more openness on the part of gay people themselves. While few Thai families would welcome the idea of a gay son or daughter, there is no deep-rooted cultural or religious stigma attached and relatively little social disapproval as long as it does not become too public (especially if the son or daughter gets married and produces children, as often happens). Even transvestites have always had a place in traditional society, playing prominent roles in folk theatre and taking part in most festivals. A few years ago, a transvestite boxer became a brief sensation (until he decided to have a sex operation and became a not-so-good singer instead), and a volleyball team composed largely of transvestites achieved fame by winning a national championship (and became the subject of a popular Thai film). Gay bars and massage parlours are almost as common as straight ones and attract as many lonely Westerners in search of love.

Such openness, in the sense of public discussion, is relatively recent and, like political awareness, probably a response to similar developments in other parts of the world; it may or may not be proof of any actual increase in the number of homosexuals. Some interesting facets have been revealed, though. For instance, Dr Peter Jackson, an Australian academic who has made Thai homosexuality his field of study, claims that the word *gay* was taken up in the mid-'60s following the murder of an American called Darrell Berrigan, editor of the *Bangkok World*. Berrigan was shot in the back seat of his car by a male hustler whom he unwisely picked up late one night, and the circumstances left little doubt as to what had been going on. The *World* and the *Bangkok Post*, the only two English-language papers at the time, were discreet in reporting the case.

The Thai press, on the other hand, gave it their full, lurid attention and almost at once encountered a linguistic problem. *Kathoey*, meaning 'transvestite', was the word initially used to describe both Berrigan and his killer (who was arrested shortly afterward), but as the facts emerged, it was clear that the term was incorrect. *Kathoeys*, as everybody knew, dressed and behaved like women and were easily recognized. Yet here were two people who looked and acted like men, but preferred other men like themselves; indeed, as the reporters discovered to their professed horror, there was a whole world of such men walking around Bangkok, unsuspected by the straight majority. Various alternate terms were tried, included such composites as *kathoey phuchai* ('masculine transvestite'), but none of them seemed quite right. Eventually, 'gay' was borrowed from English, used as a noun, and the press moved on to a furious exposé of this supposedly new phenomenon, calling on the police to do something about it until other matters arose to attract their jaded readers.

But, Jackson has said, this was a watershed of sorts. 'The Berrigan case alerted the public to changes taking place in the Thai sex/gender system,' he has written, 'leading to attempts to understand the new category of gay and also to reconsider the meaning of the older category of *kathoey*.'

Bangkok is the acknowledged centre of what the Thais call *sanuk*, a term that is usually translated as 'fun' or 'pleasure', but that encompasses a good deal more than these English equivalents. A substantial part of Thai life, in fact, can be divided into two broad categories: activities that are *sanuk* and those that are not, the latter being just about the worst possible criticism of any undertaking.

Sanuk is not limited to the obvious pastimes, like games and parties; almost any activity can earn the accolade under the right circumstances. Hard work, for instance, can be *sanuk* providing that it is not routine or solitary (nothing done the same way every day is *sanuk* and neither is anything done alone, a condition Thais cannot imagine anyone voluntarily choosing with the possible exception of a few very ascetic monks and perhaps some eccentric *farangs*); so can a class in school (providing the teacher cooperates), a particular mall or market, even apparently solemn ceremonies. The ability to find *sanuk* in so many ways is an important component of Thai charm, and its abundance in Bangkok is certainly why so many of them choose to live in the city.

Why some experiences fail to meet the test is hard for an outsider to comprehend, but the evaluation is instinctive and merciless. A well-travelled Thai woman I knew went to Russia on a cultural tour, and when she returned I asked her what she thought of it. 'Not *sanuk*,' she pronounced with grim finality, as a judge might sentence a mass murderer. And with that, Russia was off the list forever as far as she was concerned.

On the other hand, one is often pleasantly surprised. Not long ago, I decided to remove a tree from my garden that was threatening to fall on my house. It was a very large tree of the *Ficus* (fig) family, with milky sap that caused an itch, and cutting it down branch by branch was clearly going to be a nasty job. I got in touch with a man who works for the municipality and who is willing to take on such chores as a way of earning extra money. He came with four assistants and a truck. For the next eight hours, they hacked and sawed away, deftly lowering bits of the tree on ropes to avoid damaging plants below. At one point, about halfway through, my servant suggested that a bottle of *mekong*, the local rice whisky, might be welcome, and we sent out for one. The whole laborious operation was accompanied by jokes and laughter; one of the workers, a tough young man who spent his days on a garbage truck, performed daring acrobatic feats on higher branches, drawing applause from a group of neighbours who had gathered to watch. When it was all over and the last piece of debris was stacked neatly on the truck, we bought another bottle of *mekong* and they departed, assuring me it had all been very *sanuk*.

For a considerable number of the tourists who come to Bangkok, of course, *sanuk* is sex, pure and simple. This has been true ever since the emergence of Patpong (and, not coincidentally, the development of mass tourism) in the 1960s, and — despite the heated protests of feminists, anti-paedophiles, AIDS activists and other groups — it will probably go on being true for the foreseeable future.

The industry has shown a tendency to specialize according to nationality and tastes. Since Japanese are more comfortable

Banglamphu, an area of Bangkok popular with backpackers.

when they can speak their own language and eat familiar food, whole streets (Taniya Road, for example) have been transformed into mini-Tokyos, totally Japanese except for the girls. Visiting Arabs have their bars along Nana Road, while other areas cater to groups from Taiwan and mainland China. A number of small alleyways off Silom Road are primarily gay. Patpong itself in recent years seems to have been aspiring to a slightly less raunchy image, with a night market that attracts family groups and open-air restaurants.

Journalists have played an important role in spreading the word. Few, even the most conscientious, have been able to resist including a colourful passage or two about the city's sex scene, and many have written about almost nothing else. For example, in *Beyond the Blue Horizon* (1986), in which he retraces the route of the old pre-war Imperial Airways service to Australia, Alexander Frater (former chief travel correspondent of the *Observer*) stays only one night in Bangkok, most of it in a Patpong bar. There, he views (and describes in detail) a 'plump, motherly-looking woman' who shoots pingpong balls out of her vagina 'with such velocity that they whistled over our heads like grapeshot'; another woman who opens a bottle of beer with the same organ; and a live show in which the male 'performed with machine-like efficiency, spinning the girl this way and that, turning her up, down and over, demonstrating so many bewildering positions and such phenomenal staying power that I began to sense a growing resentment among some of the audience'.

In deference to their politically correct audiences, these writers generally profess to be appalled by such spectacles. Thus Frater, when a man he meets in the bar suggests going off to a massage parlour, comments, 'What I had seen made any kind of erotic activity seem about as desirable as going over the Niagara Falls in a bucket.' And Pico Iyer, who in *Video Night in Kathmandu* (1988) has a lengthy chapter on the subject, says that Bangkok 'made me decidedly squeamish. Just to be exposed to such a society was, I thought, to contract a kind of social disease, just to be here was to be guilty'.

Of course, the effect, as these authors well know, is not to repel, but to make what they describe seem even more alluring to readers in faraway wintry climes. Their lurid exposés attract ever more planeloads of overweight Americans, Germans, Australians, Englishmen and Arabs, not to mention all-male tour groups of Japanese, Koreans and Taiwanese, all bent on experiencing this sexual Shangri-La for themselves and perhaps (who knows?) finding some young beauty who not only performs tricks, but who will truly love them for what they are and not for their wallets. In fact, they almost never do. Thai women who frequent bars, even the youngest of them, are supremely practical about such matters, and while they are not averse to marriage with a *farang*, it is nearly always a costly arrangement and often a disastrous one. The men who content themselves with a few weeks of mild self-deception, however, rarely complain; they have gotten more attention than they would have had back home;

nobody has rejected them with obvious scorn; it has even been *sanuk* (if you like that sort of thing).

Sex is *sanuk* for Thais, too, of course, but rarely in places like Patpong, unless they are there to hustle, wait on tables or profit in some way. They prefer their own outlets, which are certainly not in short supply, but which probably do not offer such imaginative exhibitions. In his book, Frater mentions a table of Thais at the performance he saw, but I suspect that he was mistaken; if so, they were probably the owners of the establishment or entertaining some visiting Chinese friends.

Shopping is one of the most basic sources of *sanuk*, not so much in the glossy new air-conditioned emporia (which are, in the main, the privileged preserves of children of the wealthy, hard-eyed society ladies with rigidly lacquered hair, and tourists, especially Japanese, who, it seems, can never resist an opportunity to buy another brand-name handbag or scarf), but rather in one of the public markets and, almost everywhere, along the crowded pavements.

Periodically, when I have errands to run in what to me is 'downtown', I have to walk along a few blocks of upper Silom Road, and I never cease to be amazed at what is regularly on offer at 9:00 a.m. To mention only a few things at random, I can have a key reproduced, a shirt darned and my shoes resoled; I can buy a bottle of freshly squeezed orange juice, take-out portions of several different Thai curries, a cheese sandwich, some of the deep-fried doughnuts popular with morning coffee, a selection of watches and leather goods, assorted fruits (guavas, pineapples, mangos, bananas etc.), a dozen or so different Thai sweets (among them the delectable *khanom krok*, made in a special iron pan), a lottery ticket that may win me a million *baht*, a bunch of cut orchids, an artfully fashioned little wreath made of fragrant jasmine to offer at a shrine, and, if for some reason I need it, a large block of ice from a open-front shop that has been supplying it from the same place for at least fifty years.

There are literally thousands of such pavement markets all over Bangkok, as well as even more portable kitchens that are set up with a few tables and stools wherever a likely group of customers can be found. Some appear for only a few hours, usually in the early morning, while others are more or less permanent fixtures; along Silom, there is an extensive night market aimed solely at tourists who flock to that area after dark in search of a fake Rolex and a T-shirt, as well as less tangible pleasures. Nearly all of such markets are technically illegal; every new city government since I have been in Bangkok has announced plans to eliminate them in the cause of municipal hygiene, civic order or some other lofty goal. Every one of them has failed.

In addition, there are huge general markets that offer everything from food to household goods, as well as others that specialize in particular categories. For cut flowers, brought in huge quantities by boat and truck, dedicated buyers go to Pak Klong Talad on the river, a complex maze that is at its busiest in the pre-dawn hours. Penang and Singapore markets on Rama IV Road are the places to go for bargain-priced radios, TV sets, watches and household appliances, while Bobay Market in the Thewes District offers used (as well as new) clothing. Those in search of the freshest and most exotic fruits and vegetables go to the big farmers' co-operative on Kampengphet Road, across from Chatuchak Park, which is also close to the permanent plant market where you can buy a large pot of blooming orchids for as little as 50 *baht*. There are markets, too, where you go just for singing birds, tropical fish, monks' alms bowls, pirated video tapes and computer software, spangled G-strings for bar girls and assorted items that have somehow found their way off planes flying into Don Muang Airport (together with miniature bottles of liquor, wineglasses and airline cutlery; I was once mildly alarmed to see a life preserver).

Two of the city's oldest markets still thrive in Chinatown. One of the busiest is Sampheng, a covered lane running for seven claustrophobic blocks with wares roughly grouped into categories. One stretch, for instance, is devoted to nothing but cooking utensils, both traditional and modern, others to musical instruments, buttons, gold chains and labels for designer clothes. I have always been fascinated by the section selling small souvenirs traditionally given to guests at wedding receptions, mostly conventional enough – key rings, ceramic dolls and the like – but sometimes genuine novelties, like the little gold teeth a shop owner told me had been ordered by a dentist and his wife.

Also in the same area, and also of long standing, is Pahurat, the cloth market, largely run by Indians who form a sizeable community of their own in Bangkok. (And an influential one, too; steadily over the last twenty years or so, they have moved into more affluent parts of the city, opening tailor's shops, acquiring hotels and other prime pieces of real estate, and, in several cases, amassing large fortunes.)

Everybody's favourite market, and the most *sanuk* of all, is the Weekend Market. When I first arrived, this was still being held at Sanam Luang, the oval field across from the royal palace, and while the backdrop of gilded spires was incomparably splendid, it was a nightmare from the standpoint of traffic and parking. In the early 1980s, amid a good deal of protest from both vendors and buyers, the market was moved out to Chatuchak Park on the road leading to the airport. Pessimists predicted that this would be the end of it, for who would be willing to travel all that way (or so it seemed in those days) just to shop?

Distance proved no deterrent, however. Covering more than 30 acres and containing around six thousand stalls, the market is open from early Saturday morning until Sunday evening and offers an even more mind-boggling variety than in its Sanam Luang days. One section is devoted to food, of course, displayed with great artistic skill (pyramids of scarlet chilli peppers, mountains of purple mangosteen, cartwheels of dried cuttlefish), while others offer clothing, leather goods, folk crafts, imitation Ming porcelain, teakwood furniture, potted plants, toys, army surplus goods, textiles old and new, and tape cassettes, to mention only a few. It is hot, noisy and always crowded, and nobody would dream of paying the first price asked for anything, since bargaining is considered an important part of shopping *sanuk*. It is also an art that I have never mastered. A Thai friend who often goes with me to buy plants gets so exasperated with my willingness to pay whatever I consider to be a reasonable price that he insists that I merely nod in the direction of what I want and leave the rest to him. Lengthy negotiations ensue, and, after standing in the sweltering sun for a long time, he triumphantly announces that the price has come down by 5 or 10 *baht*.

When Bangkok people are not shopping, they seem to be eating, at almost any hour. Many sidewalk vendors offer some kind of quick snack, from a slice of fresh guava seasoned with salt and chillis to a complex bowl of noodles prepared in a matter of minutes, and the urge to consume one of these appears to have nothing to do with normal mealtimes.

Once when I lived next door to a private hospital, a plump, smiling woman appeared one morning with a portable noodle stand and set up business in the narrow street outside. Day by day it expanded, until eventually it had six tables with stools and sunshades filling a good quarter of the road. There were frequent traffic jams. An ambulance got stuck, and the patient had to be carried on a stretcher the rest of the way, past snacking nurses. But nobody complained, least of all the local policemen who lunched there daily; it had become a part of the neighbourhood scene, and is still there, fifteen years later.

Similar establishments spring up outside factories and construction sites (or at least used to, when such sites were still busy), specializing in *gai yang* (barbecued chicken), *som tam* (green papaya salad) and other dishes likely to find favour with the predominantly north-eastern workers; outside government offices, where they can be assured of regular customers among the lower-ranking employees; down narrow alleyways, in parking lots — almost anywhere, in fact, that looks promising.

Some of these simple places acquire widespread fame for their skill at preparing certain dishes. A columnist for the *Bangkok Post*, regarded as perhaps the leading authority on local food, regularly writes glowing reviews of their creations, though he often has difficulty explaining exactly where they are. It is also not uncommon to see a sleek new Mercedes Benz or two parked nearby and their well-dressed owners sharing the premises with humble regulars; nothing is more likely to bring out the true democratic spirit of the Thais than the prospect of a culinary treat.

Most of the food served in these places is either basically Chinese (though often in adapted forms) or regional (northern, north-eastern and, in a few cases, southern). More refined Thai cooking, sometimes referred to as 'royal cuisine', served in equally refined surroundings, is a relatively recent addition to the city scene. Forty years ago, almost no restaurants offered it; affluent Thais preferred Chinese or Western when they ate out, explaining that only well-staffed homes were capable of all the time-consuming and painstaking preparations that a proper Thai meal required. Aristocratic homes were well staffed in those days; the kitchen of one Thai princess with whom I used to lunch regularly had four cooks, one responsible only for sweets, as well as a small army of assistants; guests generally received a complete Western meal followed by a complete Thai one.

Today, of course, that has changed along with so much else. Thai food has become an international phenomenon (even though much of what is served in Los Angeles and London is likely to be Lao, or at least north-eastern food, adapted for *farang* palates), and tourists have become more discriminating, while fewer local homes have the necessary hands for all that skilled work. As a result, every hotel now has its Thai outlet and there are countless elegant restaurants outside, where the fare is served on celadon plates, adorned with exquisitely carved fruits and vegetables that are themselves minor works of perishable art.

Western food, too, has become popular with ordinary Thais, especially younger ones. This was not the case 40 years ago, when – outside hotels like the Oriental and the Erawan – the choice was extremely limited. Though I am sure that there must have been others, I remember only a handful; nearly everybody in the expatriate community had cooks in those days and entertained at home, rarely venturing out for dinner. In an old, vine-encrusted house that seemed in danger of imminent collapse, a Hungarian émigré offered goulash and delectable chocolate cake prepared by his mother (who also told fortunes); a Filipina married to a Thai had a place that specialized in American-style sandwiches and baked goods; on pre-boom Patpong, a Japanese who had been in the hotel business attracted visiting foreign journalists with sizzling steaks and a boozy atmosphere. That was about the extent of it. Then, gradually at first but then more rapidly, a much broader world opened up. Suddenly, there were French restaurants, then German, Danish, Mexican, Lebanese and Italian ones; for a short time, there was even a kosher delicatessen.

Fast food was slower to catch on. The British chain Wimpy's opened and quickly closed, as did a few brave pizza pioneers who defied the popular belief that Thais would simply not eat cheese in any form. By the late '70s, however, mainly in Bangkok, a new generation had grown up with tastes often acquired abroad and money to spend. Pizza parlours became the new rage, cheese notwithstanding, along with Kentucky Fried Chicken, McDonalds, Burger King, Starbucks, Chicken Nuggets and all of the other symbols of our global age. These were effortlessly absorbed into Bangkok's polymorphous street life, complementing, though by no means replacing, the traditional noodle shops and sidewalk vendors.

If you come into Bangkok by train (as not many do these days), you will catch a glimpse of another aspect of the city, one largely hidden from the average visitor and even from many residents. Jammed together on both sides of the tracks, sometimes perilously close, is a grim collection of flimsy shacks assembled from waste wood, cardboard and sheets of rusting corrugated iron, linked to the outside world by rickety board-walks over pools of stagnant black water. Bold rats can be seen scampering through piles of garbage, along with mangy dogs and swarms of half-naked children, some of whom may wave enthusiastically at the passing carriages.

Beginning in the 1950s and continuing more or less unchecked until the financial disasters of the late '90s slowed it down, Thailand experienced a mass migration from rural areas to the country's one really large city, the one place that might possibly offer escape from crop failures, greedy money lenders or simple boredom. Many (perhaps the majority) of these migrants arrived with few or no skills, little education and the ability to earn at best a meagre income. They ended up either paying a small rent to a slum landlord or, like those along the railway track, squatting on somebody else's property in a slum of their own creation. Most live on land owned by huge, impersonal agencies like the State Railways, the Port Authority, and the Thai Tobacco Monopoly, all of which have extensive, under-utilized tracts in the heart of the city. The largest concentration, estimated at over a 100,000 (though nobody knows for sure), live on Port Authority land at Klong Toey, a vast shanty-town on a swampy stretch near the river that is rarely entered by outsiders.

Some of the Klong Toey squatters manage to find low-paying work at the port or construction sites. Others sell food or home-made crafts along the pavements, sift through garbage in search of anything that might be recycled, become prostitutes, petty criminals or beggars (though there are remarkably few of the latter in Bangkok), escape reality through drugs (especially amphetamines, known in Thai as *ya ba*, 'crazy medicine') or homemade liquor, and suffer from skin rashes, malnutrition, tuberculosis, AIDS and all of the other afflictions of the poor. Until the 1970s, scarcely any attention was paid to this enormous population, which one researcher accurately labelled 'an unrecognized country'. The press took note of them only when

132

Klong Toey slum.

some disaster struck, like devastating fires that sometimes started accidentally and sometimes were set on purpose by hired arsonists in an effort to drive the squatters elsewhere. No charity balls or fashion shows – those staples of Thai society – were organized on behalf of the Klong Toey squatters; no social workers or medical teams visited them; the government, it seemed, was far more concerned with the problems of the hill tribes who live in the mountains of the far north than with these unfortunates literally on its doorstep.

Real awareness of such people first came with the rising social consciousness of the early 1970s and was given a rare human face when a genuine leader emerged from the slum itself in the unlikely person of a slight, soft-spoken school-teacher in her twenties named Prateep Ungsongtham. She was born in Klong Toey to a Chinese fisherman and his Thai wife, who had come from a small provincial town on the gulf to seek their fortunes, and, like most squatter children, she would normally have been denied even the most elementary

133

schooling. To qualify for a government school, a child has to have a birth certificate, but to get such a document the parents have to live in a registered house; the problem, of course, was that none of the slum houses were, or could be, registered, since that would imply legal ownership of the land.

The great majority of Klong Toey's families accepted this as merely another fact of slum life, along with the crime, the lack of sanitation and the constant threat of eviction. Prateep's mother was an exception. She was determined to give her daughter at least the rudiments of an education, and to do so she was willing to somehow scrape together the necessary money to send her to a cheap private school on the fringe of the slum. After four years, though, the funds ran out, and Prateep was back in the alleyways compelled to earn a living. This she did by packing firecrackers for 1 *baht* a day, scraping the rust off the hulls of ships in the port and looking through a nearby dump for things that might be resold. Much later, when she spoke to people about this period of her life, she did so in a matter-of-fact way, as though such jobs were perfectly normal for an undersized girl of ten. And they were, of course, and still are, in Klong Toey; it was how most of her contemporaries were spending their time.

But there was a difference in Prateep's case. Her brief exposure to school had fired her with a determination to go back, and to that end she began to put aside a small part of her earnings. By the time she was fifteen, she had saved enough to enroll in an evening school for adults, where she managed to complete six years of study in only two and a half. Still short of her eighteenth birthday, she then entered evening classes at a teacher's training college. Finally, certificate in hand, she turned one small room of the family shack into a sort of day-care centre for young children of working parents, some of whom paid her a *baht* a day for the service. From 29 the first week, enrolment rose to 60 by the end of the second month.

In the beginning, the curriculum amounted to little more than reading aloud from Thai storybooks. Gradually, though, lessons in reading and writing were introduced, and, almost without realizing it, Prateep found herself running a proper school. It was illegal, of course, since it did not have permission from either the Bangkok Municipality Administration or the Ministry of Education. A representative from the latter showed up one day, in fact, and issued a vague warning, as did a visitor from the Welfare Department who had heard about the school. But no further word was received from these two emissaries, and Prateep's classes might have continued unnoticed by the outside world had it not been for a crisis that arose towards the end of 1972.

The Port Authority informed Prateep and some two thousand of her neighbours that the area in which they lived – officially designated as Block 12 – was required for 'development' and that they would have to leave. There was consternation, of course, and a certain amount of disorganized protest. But even when squatters have inhabited an area for upward of 30 years, as many in Klong Toey had, they have no legal rights in Thailand. No-one paid much attention until a reporter from the *Bangkok Post* happened to hear about it, saw the possible makings of a good story and went to call on Prateep shortly before the Port Authority's deadline for evacuation.

Perhaps it was merely that the times were right for a heroine of the very lowest class. Or perhaps the story would have been sure-fire at any time, containing as it did all of the classic ingredients and ending with the moist-eyed tribute: 'Sixty slum children and a dedicated teacher barely out of her teens ... *Khun Kru, chok dee na krap* ["Good luck, Miss Teacher"]!' Prateep herself was quoted as saying,

If legal action is taken against me I shall be glad to face the consequences, for what I am doing is morally right. But if I am forced to closed down my day school because of the law, then all I will be able to do is cry because I cannot afford to register it.

135

Response to the article was gratifyingly swift. Donations to the school poured in, most from individual readers but some from more influential sources like foreign embassies as well as the Bangkok Bank, whose officers included several powerful citizens. Students from Thammasat University, headquarters of the anti-government protest movement then building to a climax, showed up as volunteer teachers. And the press, both Thai and English-language, eagerly reported every development.

Cast in the role of villain, the Port Authority compromised. The residents of Block 12 would still have to move, but they could relocate to some empty land not yet needed, further back in the slum. The move turned into a show of unprecedented slum solidarity. The three-hundred-odd families involved selected representatives to divide the new area into housing sites, and when the time came they helped one another take down the old shacks and reassemble them. Half an acre was reserved on which to build a real school for the young teacher, now regarded as a leader.

The school's first building – a one-storey, three-room structure for first and second graders – opened in 1974 with 150 students and three teachers, among them, of course, Prateep. Over the next few years, three other buildings were added, offering classes through the sixth grade as well as a kindergarten and vocational training classes for adults. In 1976 the Bangkok Municipality Administration finally decided to overlook the birth-certificate requirement and granted the school official recognition, agreeing to pay the salaries of some of the teachers. Prateep decided to call it the Pattana (Development) Village Community School.

Despite her growing fame, however, none of this was accomplished easily. The Bangkok Bank, the Japanese embassy, the Rotary Club, the American Women's Club of Thailand and other groups might regard the project as worthy of support; the press might call her 'the slum angel' and make her name familiar to every newspaper reader; but even in the days of democratic ferment following the 1973 revolution, officialdom remained wary. For example, when five tons of clothing donated by Japanese foundations came addressed to Prateep, it was declared dutiable and placed in a warehouse for six months while storage bills mounted to more than 9,000 *baht*. Another Japanese donation, this one in cash totalling $10,000, was presented not to Prateep but to the Municipality Administration for the purpose of helping the school; it went into a general education fund and never reached Klong Toey at all. Meanwhile, the Port Authority issued periodic reminders that the whole settlement was illegal and might be evicted any time.

Prateep met these and other challenges with the weapon that had first brought her to prominence – exposure in the popular press. Between 1973 and the bloody coup of 1976, Thai newspapers were quick to attack anything that smelled of official oppression, and the slum school provided an ideal opportunity to remind readers of what the urban poor had to endure. On the other hand, Prateep was shrewd enough not to allow her cause to become too closely identified with the leftist movement. Some Thammasat students, it was rumoured, tried to use the school as a focal point for radicalizing the slum people. If true, they failed in the effort, and Prateep retained her image of being above politics, one that enabled her to survive the events of 1976 more or less unscathed. In 1978 she was awarded the Ramon Magsaysay Award for Public Service, Asia's equivalent of the Nobel Prize, becoming the eighth Thai and the youngest of any nationality to do so. The Queen of Thailand sent flowers and a personal message of congratulations. In 1980, at the annual Teacher's Day celebrations, Prateep was named the most outstanding teacher in the country by her old opponent the Ministry of Education and given an award of 5,000 *baht*. In 1981 Prime Minister Prem Tinsulanonda made a surprise visit to five of Bangkok's major slums to get what the press called 'a firsthand look at the living conditions'; one of his briefings took place in Prateep's schoolyard.

Having married one of the Japanese volunteers who came to help, Prateep and the school are still there. So are other signs of the new public awareness she brought to Klong Toey, such as a home for orphans suffering from HIV (founded by a Catholic priest) and various other welfare projects. But Klong Toey and all the other slums are still there, too, reminders of another Bangkok that exists like a permanent blight just beyond its flashy façade.

Though it might not be readily apparent to visitors, Bangkok is a city of non-stop prayer. At any given moment day or night, thousands of its residents are devoutly pleading with some unseen force to grant their most urgent wishes.

Surprisingly few do so in the several hundred *wats* that are such a notable architectural feature of the city, especially in older sections. On one of the major Buddhist holidays, like Visaka Puja (which celebrates the Buddha's birth, enlightenment and death) or Makka Puja (commemorating the miraculous assembly of 1,250 disciples who gathered spontaneously to pay homage to him), the temples will indeed be crowded with people who form processions to walk three times around the main building with lighted candles in their hands. And there are nearly always pious groups at the Temple of the Emerald Buddha, the most sacred in all the kingdom, and sometimes at others when a particularly revered monk delivers a sermon. Go on an ordinary day, though, to even the most celebrated like Wat Benchamabopit, Wat Suthat and Wat Po, and apart from resident monks, you are likely to see only a few old men and women, along with the inevitable tourists and guides.

This is not necessarily an indication that Buddhism is losing strength in Bangkok, though some would assert that it is; the Thai press seems particularly to relish the exposing of monks who break their vow of celibacy, or who show an un-Buddhist fondness for such worldly items as credit cards, land-title deeds and expensive automobiles. It is more likely, however, that the sparse attendance is one of the inevitable consequences of city life. There is just not enough time for hard-working people to get to a *wat* on anything like a regular basis, much less for them to use one as a centre of social and spiritual life in the way that villagers do. Instead, most homes have a small 'Buddha room' or, often, merely an altar where images are kept and daily prayers are said by family members.

Even so, far more prayers are being offered at the countless non-Buddhist shrines that can be found in every part of Bangkok, usually just a short walk from wherever one is working or living. On his first day in office, a new minister of finance was reported to have prayed for guidance at no fewer than six, all of them somewhere within or near the ministry grounds and none of them dedicated to the faith he and 95 per cent of his fellow Thais profess to follow. These represent a bewildering assortment of deities that have been effortlessly adopted by the tolerant Thais, some predating Buddhism and others comparatively new. Just about every compound, whether residential, commercial or official, for instance, contains a small structure that serves as the symbolic residence of the guardian spirit of that particular bit of territory. Traditionally, these are simple little wooden Thai-style houses, but in status-conscious Bangkok, with its fondness for display, they are more likely to be elaborately decorated cement and stucco affairs, strongly suggestive of religious or royal architecture. In either case, they are always raised up off the ground on posts, usually at the outer edge of a property, and kept supplied with frequent offerings of fresh flowers, incense sticks and tidbits of food, as well as figurines representing human and animal attendants. Prayers are offered on a daily basis by those who live and work in the compound but also often by outsiders in such places as hospitals, large banks and government offices.

Among Bangkok's innumerable public shrines, perhaps the oldest is Lak Muang, the 'city pillar' installed by King Rama I just outside the walls of his palace. Sheltered by an ornate pavilion, this is a tall column with a bulbous top, described in many European accounts as an obvious phallic symbol derived from the Shiva-linga of Hinduism. A study by an Australian anthropologist, however, casts doubt on this easy assumption. He notes that 'what is "obviously" a phallus in Western Europe need not necessarily be so in Thailand'; Thais, he found, tend to compare the pillar to a plant such as a lotus bud or the tip of a banana blossom. Whatever its origins, the 'city pillar' is noted for its power to grant such wishes as a winning lottery number, a passing grade for nearby Thammasat University students, success in a new business venture or merely relief from a general run of bad luck. In exchange, petitioners promise various rewards – a roasted chicken, perhaps, or a pig's head, a dozen or more hard-boiled eggs, a bottle of whisky, sometimes cash and jewellery. The War Veterans Association, which manages the shrine, has installed a vault for the valuables donated, using the funds for maintenance and charity.

Not far away, outside Saranrom Palace, a fanciful structure that was built as a residence for Rama VI when he was Crown Prince and that now houses part of the Ministry of Foreign Affairs, stands a different kind of shrine, this one in the form of a large pig. Known as Chao Mae Moo, 'The Divine Pig', it attracts mostly women who apply flakes of gold leaf to its ample sides, which are now heavily encrusted. Probably few of these present-day devotees are aware that the pig was erected in honour of Chulalongkorn's Queen Saowapa Pongsri, who was born on 1 January 1863, the Day of the Waning Moon in the the Year of the Pig. Many royal statues and memorials have acquired such semi-religious status, especially those associated with Chulalongkorn.

Of more recent origin is the shrine at Rajprasong near the Grand Hyatt Erawan Hotel, diagonally across from the gigantic (and unfinished) World Trade Centre. This dates back to the late '50s when the original Erawan Hotel, owned and managed by the government, was being built. Assorted accidents plagued

Offerings at the Erawan shrine.

workers during construction, delaying the project; one even occurred far from the site when a ship bringing a cargo of Italian marble for the lobby sank mysteriously. In Thailand, such accumulated calamities are rarely viewed as mere coincidence, and before long it was suggested that responsibility might lie with malign forces beyond simple human fallibility. Since Erawan, the name selected for the hotel, was the three-headed elephant on which Brahma traditionally rode, it seemed logical to dedicate a shrine to that particular god, already well established in the Thai pantheon. This was done in 1955; the disrupting mishaps ceased (to no-one's great surprise), and the hotel opened the following year.

But that was only the beginning. The shrine proved even more popular with the general public than with Erawan employees, and the corner soon became one of the liveliest places in Bangkok. So many people come at all hours that the enclosure has been enlarged several times, most recently when the old hotel was replaced by a new and far grander establishment. A cultural note may be injected here. The original Erawan had been built in a bastardized style sometimes described as 'modern Thai', popular in the '50s and '60s, which meant that it added a few decorative Thai features to an otherwise bland, box-like modern structure. A group of local architects nevertheless protested loudly against the demolition of what they described as a treasured specimen of cultural heritage. They were ignored, of course, as they always are when a valuable piece of real estate is at issue. The new Erawan, in turn, was a perfect reflection of its time, with towering Corinthian columns, acres of tinted glass, a pair of massive bronze three-headed elephants at the entrance and almost no Thai features at all.

Taxi drivers offer a quick, sometimes perilous prayer to the Erawan shrine as they speed past, and countless wooden elephants, large and small, along with mountains of floral wreaths, pile up around it, so many that they have to be regularly cleaned out to make room for more. As the resident god is said to be especially fond of pretty dancing girls, a semi-permanent troop of them is available to perform in the glittery costumes of the Thai classical dance. Rumour claims that some non-professional supplicants have danced bare-breasted there late at night, and at least one is supposed to have done so naked in the early hours of the morning.

I developed a close relationship with a little-known shrine back in the 1960s, when I moved into a house on Klong Saen Saeb, at the end of a shady lane beside the British Embassy. A fence ran along one side of my compound, and beyond it grew a dense, weedy mini-jungle, which raised at least two problems. One was aesthetic; I had by that time become an enthusiastic gardener, and the neighbouring tangle seemed an unhappy contrast to the neat beds and smooth lawn I was laying out in what was, for Bangkok, an unusually generous space. The other was more practical; assorted reptiles, including cobras and a nasty little red-tailed viper, frequently wandered out of that congenial home and turned up on my doorstep.

When I presented my difficulties to my landlady, she was sympathetic but explained that the area had been fenced off for a reason. In one part of the jungle, overlooking the canal, there was a shrine, the abode of a female spirit called Chao Mae Tuptim. It had formerly stood at the base of a huge tree of the *Ficus* family, always a popular site for shrines because of the twisting aerial roots that created little grottoes considered to be natural spiritual residences. The tree had fallen down and been washed away in a famous flood during the war years, but the shrine survived, visited regularly by some of the boat-people who passed. She herself, she assured me, was very modern about such matters; still, she preferred not to offend those who did believe and felt that the shrine should continue to be accessible.

We reached a compromise, as one usually does in Thailand. The fence would remain, but I could clear the unsightly growth and turn it into a sort of mini-park, leaving Chao Mae Tuptim's

Shrine in the grounds of the Hilton Hotel.

abode available not only to supplicants who might want to come by water but also to others, for whom a special gate would be built on the land side.

As the tropical creepers and waist-high grass were removed (and, incidentally, a six-foot python roused from sleep), an interesting fact came to light. (Interesting to me, that is; I am sure that my landlady and others knew it all along.) The offerings that had been left at the shrine, some of them years before, consisted almost solely of phalluses that by no stretch of the imagination could have been taken for lotuses or banana blossoms. They were everywhere, large and small, crude and refined, bright with red paint or riddled with termites like some awful warning of venereal disease, fashioned from a variety of materials. Exactly why this was so I never completely understood. Most people, at least my *farang* friends, assumed that it had something to with sex, probably a desire for children, but those who actually came with offerings assured me this was usually not the case. The spirit's powers were far broader, they said; in addition to helping the barren and impotent, she could grant all kinds of wishes, though in return she had a marked preference for phallic objects.

These certainly accumulated rapidly after my landscaping effort was completed and the shrine became more accessible. One offering was gigantic, made of terrazzo, with two life-sized legs to support it, while another appeared in the form of a jumbo jet, complete with the Thai Airways logo. Boat traffic along Klong Saen Saeb began to decline around that time, but increasing numbers of visitors came by land, among them occasional *farangs*. An American men's magazine devoted several colour pages to the offerings, and the final chapter of the book (though not the movie) version of *Emmanuelle* takes place there. Photographers would show up while I was working in the garden, claiming a keen interest in anthropology.

In time, my house was torn down to make way for the Hilton International Hotel. The shrine was spared, though (indeed, most of the staff made a point of praying there on the day the hotel opened) and still stands with all of its offerings in a secluded corner of the large garden. (So do several of the trees I planted nearby to mark the final resting places of various pets; I go from time to time to pay homage to Chao Mae Tuptim and also to Lily, Tiger, Lenny and other well-remembered friends.)

Two hundred and twenty years after it was founded by King Rama I, 70 years after the end of the absolute monarchy, Bangkok remains a royal capital. This is apparent from portraits of the King and Queen that hang prominently in even the most humble noodle shop, and one becomes even more aware of it on various annual occasions. A week or so before the King's Birthday, on 5 December, for instance, enormous portraits of His Majesty go up in front of both government and commercial buildings, Ratchadamnoen Avenue is festooned with decorations, and many private homes display the Thai flag; on the day itself, the King appears on television, delivering an address to the nation. There are other regular royal events, among them the Queen's Birthday in August, Chakri Day in April, Coronation Day in May, the trooping of the colours in November outside the old Dusit Throne Hall and the ritual changing of the Emerald Buddha's robes by the King at the beginning of each season (rainy, cool and hot).

In addition, some member of the royal family traditionally hands out degrees to each graduate of the older universities, as well as to the military academy. (The King used to do this himself, but the current number of graduates – at Chulalongkorn University, the ceremony stretches out over three days – makes it too much of a physical strain.) They also preside at weddings, at the funerals of prominent people and at assorted charity functions to raise funds for royal projects. News of these and other activities is featured nightly on all of the local television stations.

Rarer, and considerably more elaborate, are royal cremations, still held at Sanam Luang outside the Grand Palace. There have been only two of these in recent years, one in 1985 for Queen Rambhai Barni, widow of King Rama VII, and one in 1996 for the mother of the present King, who had been born a commoner but rose to become one of the most beloved figures in Thailand. On both occasions, identical in most details to ones held over a century ago, a spectacular golden pyre was erected in the field, and ancient chariots (the chief one weighing 36 tons and requiring 216 men to pull it) took part in the procession. Almost as rare these days are Royal Barge Processions along the Chao Phraya River, in which the King goes to present robes to the monks of Wat Arun; the last was held in 1996, as part of the celebration of his golden jubilee.

Thailand has a very strict *lèse-majesté* law forbidding public criticism of members of the royal family, but it is seldom needed, especially with regard to the King himself, who despite his limited constitutional powers is the most revered member of his dynasty since the great Chulalongkorn. Though an enthusiastic and talented jazz musician (a song he composed was once used in a Broadway musical), he determined early in his reign to devote himself to good works and has done so with extraordinary success. For the most part, these have been outside Bangkok. He has visited remote villages in every province of the country and has initiated over two thousand 'royally suggested' projects covering everything from water conservation and artificial rainmaking to flood control and the introduction of new crops.

Such efforts have given the monarchy a new image and made it a potent moral force in Thai society, something above the usually sordid political struggles that both leaders and ordinary people feel they can turn to in times of turmoil. As we have seen, the students of 1973 carried pictures of the royal family in their mass demonstrations, and it was the King who eventually persuaded the chief targets to leave the country. In 1992, when violence again broke out between pro-democracy advocates and military troops, television viewers were treated to the sight of the leaders of both factions kneeling to receive his advice.

How much of this devotion is due to the individual and how much to the institution remains to be seen, but there can be no doubt that most Thais continue to view the monarchy as an essential part of the social structure.

A year or so ago, an old American friend came for her first visit to Bangkok. She insisted on staying at the Oriental Hotel, still a favourite despite its somewhat inconvenient location, and on her second night came to me for dinner, arriving an hour late thanks to the traffic. (The new elevated expressways are wonderful for cutting travel time to many parts of the city, including the airport, but none of them, alas, provides a direct route between the Oriental and my area.)

She made a few polite remarks about my small garden and my 'Asian things', but, barely into her second drink, could not resist saying what was obviously much on her mind: 'I can see you have a nice little refuge here, but I assume you have to go out some time and how can you *live* in such a place? The traffic! The pollution! The ugliness! It *must* have been very different when you decided to make it your home.' I made my usual responses, which by now have become more or less automatic. Yes, it was very different 40 years ago; one adjusts more easily to changes when one lives in the middle of them; I work at home, so I have do not have to deal with the traffic and pollution on a daily basis.

None of what I said was true, or at least not wholly so. Of course, Bangkok *was* different when I came, though not in the romantic way I am sure she meant. It was smaller, for instance, in both size and population, but it was just as ugly, with the same basic row-shop architecture, the same unsightly tangle of electric wires everywhere, the same crowded, potholed pavements that make walking a hazardous adventure. There were more of the *klongs* that were such a feature of early descriptions – 'the Venice of the East' was a popular phrase in many of them — but, with a few exceptions, they had long been little more than open sewers. Fewer cars and buses naturally made for less traffic but even so, it managed to be nightmarish because even major streets were much narrower and likely to disappear under water with even a moderate monsoon rain. And though she might have looked back on it later with a certain nostalgia (as I occasionally do), I doubt my friend would really have enjoyed the lack of air conditioning, gas cookers, telephones and a reliable supply of electricity.

Nor have I truly been unaware of all of the city's dramatic transformations in recent years. For a time in the early '90s, it seemed that a new highrise went up every month or so even in my own once-quiet neighbourhood, and I had to change the landmarks on the map to guide strangers to my house so often that I gave up the idea of producing it in semi-permanent printed form. The financial collapse of 1997 put an end to such overnight transformations, but I am sure that this is only temporary; one thing one learns in Bangkok is to expect, and accept, drastic changes, usually for the worse.

But I did not want to go into all that because I knew it would have been a waste of time. My friend was not an unsophisticated woman who thought it odd to take up permanent residence abroad; I am sure that she would have understood it if I had chosen orderly, green Singapore, perhaps even brash, greedy Hong Kong. She just was not the type to respond favourably to Bangkok's peculiar appeal and could not have become so even after prolonged exposure. Those expatriates who do respond (more often men than women) favourably are a varied lot, impossible to categorize with any precision, although paradoxically the number seems to be increasing even as the less attractive aspects of Bangkok life receive more widespread attention.

Many originally came because the city offered, or seemed to offer, a significant contrast with an unsatisfactory place of origin. In his collection of essays called *The Missionary and the Libertine* (1996), Ian Buruma comments:

> It is easy to imagine the giddy sense of freedom felt by Englishmen from rainy northern towns, or Americans from God-fearing midwestern plains, when they came to Japan, or Thailand, or Ceylon, or wherever their idea of Arcadia happened to be. Because local restraints did not apply to them, and they were far from home, everything seemed suddenly possible.

That Arcadian freedom has often been of a sexual nature, as countless trashy novels continue to assert, though I suspect today that it is only part of the reason. Bangkok is indeed a very tolerant place, but not all that much more so than New York, San Francisco or London; sexual repression is now easy enough to escape without going half-way around the world. I think that there has to be something else a bit more complex to make someone want to see out the rest of his days here; after all (though admittedly I may be wrong about this), one cannot really spend year after year on a barstool or in bed.

For some, perhaps, it is the eternal lure of self-invention. As Anna Leonowens discovered, *farangs* tend to be taken at face value, and few Thais are apt to probe too deeply into such matters as family origins or educational credentials. An ambitious German can easily add a 'von' to his name, a French piano player can claim noble ancestry, an American businessman can claim all sorts of imaginary academic and social distinctions; no-one really cares, and some are undoubtedly impressed. Thais, too, in fact, have been known to explore the possibilities of such an easy-going atmosphere. There was one who regularly crashed grander functions at the better hotels, wearing an obvious hairpiece and a good deal of make-up. He told other guests that he was of royal birth, which was true, and that he owned large pieces of prime real estate all over Bangkok, which was not. Local people treated him as something of a joke, saying that his presence was a sure indication that the event was of true social consequence. Some visitors, however, took him at his word, and a few are said to have handed over money for bogus title deeds. Such pretensions as a rule do no real harm, except perhaps to the pretenders themselves when, once in a blue moon, the truth accidentally emerges. Generally, though, they go on living within their new personas quite happily, often prosperously, having finally found a stage where they can act out their secret fantasies with little risk of discovery.

Some expatriates may be perversely attracted by the undercurrent of chaos that puts off so many others. They derive a strange exhilaration from living in a place where the likelihood of confusion looms at every turn, where people seem to cheerfully disobey the law whenever they can, where pedestrians are expected to share sidewalks with food vendors and motorcycles, where corruption is an assumed part of life and nothing to get unduly exercised about, where things have a disconcerting way of not being what they seem (girls turn out to be boys, and vice versa), where the very air you breathe is a constant threat to the health you are supposed to guard so assiduously. 'In the netherworld of Bangkok,' Pico Iyer has written,

> nothing was sure, nothing secure. Names changed, relations shifted, people and places evaporated. All certainties dissolved in the soft city of hard questions; it was easy to say what it wasn't, difficult to know what it was. Bangkok was a riddler who declared, in all candor, 'I am a liar.'

Carol Hollinger even enjoyed driving in the city, pronouncing the experience 'creative': 'You had to be intensely alert to avoid collision and you were not frantically bored by regimented multitudes all obeying the law rigidly and stopping because they saw red and green.'

One American, who has lived here longer than me, says that he made up his mind even before he came. Somehow, in the small California town where he was studying back in the early '50s, he happened to see a copy of the *Bangkok Post*. It featured a small story that immediately struck a chord. One of the old tram cars, it seems, had hit a pedicab, which in turn rammed into a taxi cab, which swerved and fell into a canal on top of a charcoal barge. 'I decided then and there,' he says, 'that I had to live in a place where such marvellous accidents could happen.'

Then again, as with me, the process of attraction may be a gradual one, a slow accretion of things that you are scarcely aware of at the time, a bit like growing old. The easy ways and tolerant attitudes may have been beguiling, but I do not think that I intended to stay forever in Bangkok when I first moved here. I saw it instead as a timely opportunity to sort out various personal matters in an unfamiliar atmosphere; a few years, perhaps, and then I would go back to reality, or to what I believed to be reality.

Then weeks, months, whole years passed, during which new bonds were forged, new habits formed, new interests acquired, without my being quite aware of their significance. In retrospect it all seems to have happened rapidly, but in fact it was four years before I went back 'home' for a visit and realized for the first time that perhaps Bangkok had become more than just a temporary refuge. It was a curious experience. I still vividly remember my unease among people I had known for most of my life ('How much longer are you going to stay over there?' 'Oh, I don't know'), the strange, irrational panic that made me examine my return ticket at regular intervals to make sure that it was all in order, the flood of blessed relief and happiness that swept over me when the plane actually took off from San Francisco and headed back across the Pacific. Still, it took a couple of further visits before I knew beyond any doubt that I had found my home.

Though by now I am what Eudora Welty once described as 'underfoot locally', with the established commitments and routine activities that felicitous phrase implies, Bangkok has never lost its ability to surprise and delight, occasionally to shock and dismay, but never to bore me for any length of time. I may feel a momentary depression when, for some reason, I have to go to one of those newer suburban areas, with their grim row-shops and largely empty streets, but I can quickly dispel it by going to other parts of the city where there is always something to catch my eye and stir my curiosity.

That elephant, for example, calmly stuffing itself with grass on a vacant lot not far from where I live. (I know why it is here. Mahouts from the distant province of Surin, on the Cambodian border, bring elephants down to earn some money from tourists who feed them bananas, or from Thais, especially pregnant women, who achieve good luck by walking under them. But didn't I read in the paper a few months ago that this was now strictly forbidden? If so, how has this quite obvious specimen escaped detection?) Or that vendor on the pavement; are those golden-fried items displayed in front of her really grasshoppers? (They are indeed, regarded as a delicacy in some parts of the north-east and not bad if you focus your attention on the texture.)

A landing on the river.

Any time spent on the Chao Phraya is bound to lift my spirits, as well as summon up memories, odd bits of lore gathered over the years and, now and then, an idea for a future project. Once I explored the length of it aboard a converted teak rice barge, kindly lent by the owner, as part of research for a book. We went from where the river begins, at the confluence of the Ping and Nan rivers in Nakhon Sawan province, to Pak Nam, where it empties into the Gulf of Thailand, a trip that could be made in a few hours by car but that took us seven wonderful days, tying up at villages and temples along the way.

The brown, swirling water is not as clean as it might be, especially in the hot season, but the Chao Phraya is still very much a working river and full of varied life. The port of Klong Toey, for instance, through which most of Bangkok's imports and exports pass, is crowded with freighters from all over the world, loading, unloading, being repaired, just arriving or leaving. I never pass it without thinking of the Dutch vessel that

153

brought me here in 1960 and marvelling that I could have endured eight weeks on anything so small. A dense clump of trees just beside an ugly modern hotel conceals the old Protestant cemetery, where I have often picked my way carefully through the tall weeds in search of some tombstone – Dr Bradley's, perhaps, or that of his daughter who lived on until just before the Second World War. (Why has no-one ever done a proper book about the people who lie buried here – a lot of missionaries like Bradley, once-eminent foreign advisors to the government, anonymous sailors, a few Jewish residents whom the Catholics banned from their cemetery on Silom Road? Perhaps I will.)

Whizzing upstream in a *hong yao* 'long-tail' boat (which has a propeller attached to a long pole and a powerful outboard engine) or proceeding at a more stately pace in a smaller, less modern craft (which I prefer), I take in all of the familiar landmarks. The East Asiatic Company has moved out of the gigantic white wedding cake (*circa* 1901) that served for so long as its local headquarters, but rumour (never very reliable in Bangkok) says that the building has been registered as a historical structure and cannot be torn down or drastically altered. Behind it looms Assumption Cathedral and its élite school, where it used to be possible to get books beautifully bound in fine leather for a pittance. (Is this still true? I must check.) Then the Oriental Hotel, which in January 2001 celebrated its 125th birthday with a party for several thousand people, some of them gate-crashers eager to attend a historic occasion. Somerset Maugham, Noel Coward, John Le Carré, Gore Vidal and other eminent literary visitors have enjoyed the river view from the big old-fashioned suites on the second floor of the Author's Wing. (Vidal has a suite named after him in the newer Tower Wing, but prefers to stay in Somerset Maugham, which he says has 'more resonance'.) The French Embassy, next door, looks slightly lost in its green mini-jungle, though I remember many happy evenings in those spacious rooms with tall louvred doors; just beyond, the old Customs House looks sadly derelict, though its proportions are still splendid. (Despite years of trying, I have never succeeded in getting permission to see the interior.) The Portuguese Embassy is set back from the river, a low, solid building with arched doors and windows, built, it seems, to withstand a possible attack by the natives, proud of its long history.

On the opposite bank, between two old godowns, I catch a glimpse of the Wang Lee House, built in the 1880s by one of the Chinese immigrants who fulfilled his dream of great wealth in a new place. The extensive family does not live there now, of course, having long since moved to modern residences in more fashionable districts, but at least they have kept the building up as a sort of shrine to their ambitious ancestor. (Other once grand west-bank mansions have been less fortunate; they moulder away in weed-infested gardens, sometimes lean alarmingly this way or that; every time I go on the river, another one seems to have vanished.)

I pass under the Memorial Bridge, the first to span the Chao Phraya, which is now actually two bridges side by side, both generally packed with traffic. What I usually think about at this point, however, is not so much the bridge as a house that once stood where it reaches the Thon Buri side. Or, to be more precise, I think about Robert Hunter, the canny Scotsman who built it back in the 1820s and who played a significant role in the fortunes of the celebrated Siamese twins. It must have been just about here, where the water eddies around the bridge supports, that he first spotted what Dr Bradley described as 'a creature that appeared to have two heads, four arms, and four legs, all of which were moving in perfect harmony'. Naked children still swim off the pilings near the bank, and I always watch them carefully, hoping I too might spot a similar marvel.

Then a whole collection of landmarks, one after another, a sort of concentrated lesson in the history and legends of early Bangkok: Vichai Prasit Fort, on the site of one built in the seventeenth century to guard the river route to Ayutthaya, some of its old cannons still in place; King Taksin's Thon Buri palace, or what is left of it, curiously modest and decidedly Chinese in style; the soaring, ornately decorated towers of Wat Arun (which figures prominently in Yukio Mishima's novel *The Temple of Dawn* [1973], though for some reason he decided to relocate it just across from the Oriental); Tha Tien, the landing where all those early foreign emissaries like Sir John Bowring used to disembark on their way to royal audiences; and finally, after a collection of drab, modern buildings that make its sudden appearance all that more dramatic, the incomparable splendour of the Grand Palace and Wat Phra Keo, a sight that unfailingly thrills and removes any lingering shred of suspicion that this is just another big, noisy Asian city.

Usually on such trips, I tell the boat driver that I want to go a little further up, just beyond the Phra Pinklao Bridge. The reason is a house on the Thon Buri side that I first noticed some 30 years ago and that has lurked ever since in my imagination. It is a long structure, vaguely Palladian in style, composed of a central section and two wings, impressive without being ostentatious. I do not know who built it or when, though I would guess that it was another of those prosperous Chinese immigrants, in the latter part of the nineteenth century. I do know that it is now a Muslim-run vocational school and that, despite neglect, it is still in surprisingly good condition.

I know this because one day I took a boat across, clambered up the rotting steps to a landing and boldly went inside. The main building was being used for offices; beyond, in the same compound, was a large athletic field and a wooden classroom building, obviously added later. Several teachers were mildly surprised at my intrusion, but politely accepted my apologies and gave me permission to look around.

And what wonders I found! A magnificent central hall, still adorned with fine rosewood panels and carvings with Chinese motifs; broad corridors leading to the rooms in both wings; an enormous second-storey terrace, ideal for open-air gatherings in the cool season — all with fine views of the river just beyond a spacious cobblestoned courtyard. There are disadvantages, however. The structure is obviously subject to floods (you can see the high-water marks on the walls of lower rooms). The tiled roof leaks in places, and some of the plastered brick walls are beginning to disintegrate. The only access is by water or by a narrow alleyway behind that leads through what looks like a slum, but is more likely just an old Muslim settlement that has fallen on hard times.

But the roof could be repaired, the walls replastered; the wooden building behind could be removed and the athletic field turned into a big lotus pond, with the excavated earth used to raise the front courtyard above flood level; a new and impressive landing could be built, with a place to moor a private boat for travel along the river. It would be possible to hire a barge to transport furniture and other household goods. There are many skilled craftsman around who could restore that beautiful wood and create new elements for those motifs that are broken or missing.

An alluring idea. It is the sort of thing that could happen in Bangkok and quite often has. The sort of thing that keeps so many of us here.

Bibliography

Antonio, J., *The 1904 Traveller's Guide to Bangkok and Siam*, reprint edn (Bangkok, 1997)

Bangkok Times, The 1895 Directory for Bangkok and Siam, reprint edn (Bangkok, 1996)

Batson, Benjamin A., *The End of the Absolute Monarchy in Siam* (Singapore, 1984)

Bock, Carl, *Temples and Elephants*, reprint edn (Bangkok, 1986)

Bowring, Sir John, *The Kingdom and the People of Siam*, reprint edn (Kuala Lumpur, 1969)

Bradley, William L., *Siam Then* (New York, 1981)

Bristowe, W. S., *Louis and the King of Siam* (New York, 1982)

Caddy, Mrs Florence, *To Siam and Malaya* (London, 1889)

Chakrabongse, Prince Chula, *Lords of Life* (London, 1960)

Chu, Valentine, *Thailand Today* (New York, 1968)

Clarac, Achille, *Guide to Thailand* (Kuala Lumpur, 1981)

Conrad, Joseph, *Youth* (London, 1971)

Conyers-Keynes, S., *A White Man in Thailand* (London, 1950)

Ekachai, Sanitsuda, *Behind the Smile* (Bangkok, 1991)

Fournereau, Lucien, *Bangkok in 1892*, reprint edn (Bangkok, 1992)

Frater, Alexander, *Beyond the Blue Horizon* (London, 1987)

Gervais, Nicholas, *The Natural and Political History of the Kingdom of Siam*, reprint edn (Bangkok, 1989)

Gorer, Geoffrey, *Bali and Angkor* (Singapore, 1986)

Griswold, Alexander B., *King Mongkut of Siam* (New York, 1961)

Hollinger, Carol, *Mai Pen Rai Means Never Mind* (Boston, 1965)

Hunter, Kay, *Duet for a Lifetime* (London, 1964)

Iyer, Pico, *Video Night in Kathmandu* (New York, 1988)

Jottrand, Mr and Mrs Émile, *In Siam*, reprint edn (Bangkok, 1996)

Kaplan, Robert D., *The Ends of the Earth* (New York, 1996)

Keyes, Charles F., *Thailand: Buddhist Kingdom as Modern Nation-State*, reprint edn (Bangkok, 1989)

Klausner, William, *Reflections on Thai Culture* (Bangkok, 1993)

Landon, Margaret, *Anna and the King of Siam*, reprint edn (New York, 2000)

Leonowens, Anna, *The English Governess at the Court of Siam*, reprint edn (Bangkok, n.d.)

Lord, Donald C., *Mo Bradley and Thailand* (Grand Rapids, MI, 1969)

Maugham, W. Somerset, *The Gentleman in the Parlour* (London, 1930)

National Identity Board (Office of the Prime Minister), *Thailand in the*

2000s (Bangkok, 2001)

Neale, F. A., *Narrative of a Residence in Siam*, reprint edn (Bangkok, n.d.)

Phillips, Herbert P., *Modern Thai Literature* (Honolulu, 1987)

Reynolds, Jack, *A Woman of Bangkok*, reprint edn (Bangkok, 1985)

Smith, Malcolm, *A Physician at the Court of Siam* (Kuala Lumpur, 1982)

Smithies, Michael, ed., *Descriptions of Old Siam* (Singapore, 1995)

Stowe, Judith A. *Siam Becomes Thailand* (Honolulu, 1991)

Syamananda, Rong, *A History of Thailand* (Bangkok, 1971)

Vella, Walter F., *Chaiyo! King Vajiravudh and the Development of Thai Nationalism* (Honolulu, 1978)

Waugh, Alec, *Bangkok* (London, 1970)

Warren, William, *Jim Thompson: The Unsolved Mystery* (Singapore, 2000)

——, *Menam Chao Phraya: River of Life and Legend* (Bangkok, 1994)

Wright, Joseph J. *The Balancing Act: A History of Modern Thailand* (Oakland, CA, 1991)

Wyatt, David K., *Thailand: A Short History* (London, 1984)

Young, Edward M., *Aerial Nationalism: A History of Aviation in Thailand* (Washington, DC, 1995)

Photographic Acknowledgements

The author and publishers wish to express their thanks to the below sources of illustrative material and /or permission to reproduce it:

Courtesy of John Falconer: pp. 17 (photo: Robert Lenz & Co.), 63; Michael Leaman/Reaktion Books: pp. 19, 30, 38, 60, 62, 86, 90, 97, 99, 101, 105, 108, 113, 116, 124, 133, 141, 144, 153; British Library, London: pp. 19 [Mss Eur F111/88 (3)], 21 [Mss Eur F111/88 (8)], 36 [Mss Eur F111/88 (7)], 55 [Mss Eur F111/88 (6)], 66 [Mss Eur F111/88 (10)].